Mother Ayahuasca's Sacred Teachings: Unveiling Shiva

A Spiritual Quest Toward Enlightenment and Divine Oneness

Rudhra Hridaya

© 2025 Rudhra Hridaya. All rights reserved.

No part of this book may be reproduced, distributed, or transmitted in any form or by any means, including photocopying, recording, or other electronic or mechanical methods, without the prior written permission of the author, except in the case of brief quotations used for reviews or other non-commercial uses permitted by copyright law.

Published by: Independently Published
First Edition: January 2025
ISBN-13: 979-8-9923363-1-3

For permissions, contact:
rudhrahridaya@gmail.com

Table of Contents

Foreword	2
Dedication	6
Acknowledgments	7
Disclaimer	10
Prelude	12
Prologue	14
Chapter One: The Great Cleansing	32
Chapter Two: The Serpent God	59
Chapter Three: The Warrior's Sacrifice	83
Chapter Four: The Sacred Valley of Reflection	101
Chapter Five: A Night of Compassion	119
Chapter Six: The Cosmic Classroom	129
Chapter Seven: Lessons in Humility	156
Chapter Eight: The Warrior's Gift	166
Chapter Nine: The Warrior's Path	177
Chapter Ten: Unveiling the Lord Shiva	204
Chapter Eleven: The Gift of Unconditional Love	228
Chapter Twelve: The Healing Waters of Forgiveness	244
Chapter Thirteen: A Gift of Peace	256
Epilogue	266
About the Author	280

Foreword

It is with great honor and profound respect that I write the foreword to this profoundly moving work, *Mother Ayahuasca's Sacred Teachings: Unveiling Shiva — A Spiritual Quest Toward Enlightenment and Divine Oneness* . I have had the privilege of witnessing the transformation of the author, whose intellectual rigor and spiritual curiosity have led him on a journey that many would find both extraordinary and humbling.

When I first encountered the author, I sensed a restlessness—an unyielding thirst for meaning and a dauntless search for understanding. In our early conversations, he spoke with palpable intensity about his spiritual experiences, a pursuit that might have been met with skepticism by others; however, knowing the author, I recognized it as deeply earnest and sincere. Over the years, I have come to appreciate the path the author has walked—a path that bridges the analytical precision of scientific inquiry with the boundless, sometimes intangible mysteries of the spiritual realm. It is this very fusion of disciplines that makes this book such a unique and invaluable contribution to the subjects of spiritual discovery, intellectual evolution, and personal growth.

Through this journey, the author encountered Mother Ayahuasca, the spirit of the sacred plant brew of ancient cultures in the Americas, and found a *guru* who revealed profound truths and well-established rituals that transport the everyday self beyond the scope of profane existence and ordinary perception to the secluded plane of cosmic wholeness and erudite beauty. What began as a quest for healing and understanding of the immediate self expanded into a journey of discovery of the highest self and cosmic realization. It is from this profoundly transformative experience that this book came into existence. What the book reveals is not merely an intellectual exploration of the nature of reality or an examination of ancient spiritual traditions; concurrently, this work serves as the author's invitation to the reader to join him in a rejuvenating process of deep, unadulterated introspection and pure ideational awakening.

The author's narrative is one of personal transformation, intellectual growth, and spiritual enlightenment. The connections made between ancient teachings—particularly those from the Vedic tradition—and modern scientific inquiry are as thought-provoking as they are profound. By weaving together personal experiences with the wisdom of both Eastern and Western philosophies, the author reveals the interconnectedness of all things and, in doing so, challenges the very notions of the apparent existence of time and space. Through his journey with Mother Ayahuasca, the author has not only found answers to complex fundamental questions but has also learned how to embrace and appreciate the beauty and vastness of the unknown, which is accessible to everyone at all times.

In this book, the reader will witness a soul's progression from seeking an understanding of the mysteries of cosmic existence to embodying the very wisdom of the Ayahuasca experience. Through the author's encounters with both the Divine and the secular, the reader will begin to appreciate the complementary combination of the mesmerizing and intricate dance of Shiva and Shakti—the stillness of masculine strength and the vibrant vitality of feminine energy, each enhancing the other in a divine and sacred union. The reader will walk beside the author through moments of personal struggle and profound insight, ultimately arriving at a deep realization that we are all connected to the vast expanse of consciousness that permeates the entire universe.

This foreword has been written with the sincere hope that the book will serve not only as a reflection of the author's transformative journey but also as a beacon of light for others embarking on their quests for self-discovery and spiritual awakening. May the content of these pages inspire each reader to look beyond mere appearances and uncover the profound truths that await discovery beneath the surface.

Awakening is a universal truth available to all who seek it. It is the realization that we are already whole and connected to the infinite. In the state of awakening, there is no need for fear, no space for desire, and no cause for harm. It is a return to the natural state of peace and harmony, where we recognize our shared essence with all beings. Through this understanding, we become vessels of compassion and wisdom, living in alignment with the sacred flow of existence.

— Dr. Vasile Munteanu

Dedication

To my beloved daughter,

You are the dynamo of my life, the light that fuels my every step. Your laughter is the song that lifts my spirit, and your presence is the grounding force that keeps me connected to the essence of love. Through every challenge and triumph, you have been my constant reminder of the beauty of life's journey. This book is a testament to the wisdom, love, and inspiration you continue to bring into my world. Thank you for being my guiding star and the purest reflection of the Divine. This is for you, always.

Acknowledgments

First and foremost, I extend my deepest gratitude to **Mother Ayahuasca** , whose teachings have been the guiding light throughout this journey. Her profound wisdom and transformative presence have shaped my path in ways I never imagined possible. Each ceremony and vision has brought me closer to understanding the divine interconnectedness that binds us all. I am humbled to have been a part of this sacred journey and to have received the lessons she imparted.

To the incredible team at **Nimea Kaya Sanctuary** , thank you for providing a sacred space where profound healing and growth could occur. **Jill** , your guidance and nurturing spirit were foundational to my experience. Your commitment to creating a safe and supportive environment allowed me to delve deeply into my healing. To the **Curanderos** and **Curanderas** , your deep connection to the spirit world and the sacred icaros you shared guided me through some of the most profound experiences of my life. And to the **facilitators** , whose care and attentiveness made each ceremony feel safe, grounded, and sacred—your efforts did not go unnoticed, and I am forever grateful.

To my **spiritual brothers and sisters** at Nimea Kaya, each of you brought unique energy and presence to our shared space. The collective healing we experienced together was transformative, and I carry each of you in my heart as we continue on our separate journeys. The bond we formed in that sacred space transcends time and distance, and for that, I am deeply grateful.

A heartfelt thank you to everyone at **Spirit Quest Sanctuary** . To **Don Howard** , whose vision and wisdom created a sanctuary for seekers, I am honored to have walked through the doors of Spirit Quest. I feel blessed to have experienced the sacred energy that radiates through every corner of the land you've cultivated. To **Selva** , for continuing your father's legacy with such grace and love and for being a beacon of light throughout the retreat, I'm eternally grateful. To the **Maestros and Maestras** and all the staff at Spirit Quest, your support, energy, and guidance during the ceremonies were integral to my journey. Your deep knowledge and care allowed me to explore the depths of my soul and heal with integrity.

To my **spiritual brothers and sisters** at Spirit Quest, thank you for being part of this incredible journey. Each of you brought wisdom, love, and support, and our shared experiences in the ceremony will forever be etched in my heart. Together, we navigated the profound and often challenging paths of transformation, and for that, I am grateful beyond words.

To my dear **spiritual brother, Vishal** , thank you for walking this path with me. Our journey together, from Nimea Kaya to Spirit Quest, has deepened our bond in ways that transcend this lifetime. Your unwavering support, wisdom, and strength have been invaluable to me, and I am honored to share this spiritual brotherhood with you.

I also want to acknowledge **Dr. Vasile Munteanu** , whose mentorship and guidance provided balance and insight. You helped me navigate the intersection of spiritual awakening and academic rigor, and your belief in my quest for truth was resolute. Your deep understanding of philosophy, coupled with your compassionate guidance, has shaped not only my academic journey but my life as a whole.

Finally, to my family and friends, your love, patience, and belief in me have been a source of strength throughout this journey. Your support allowed me to take the time I needed to embark on this path, and I carry your encouragement with me every step of the way.

This book is not only a testament to my experiences but also to the guidance and wisdom shared by all those I've met along the way. To the healers, shamans, spiritual warriors, and companions I have encountered, thank you for your presence, your teachings, and your love. May this book serve as a reflection of the incredible healing, transformation, and wisdom we all continue to seek, both within ourselves and the universe.

Disclaimer

This book is based on the personal experiences, reflections, and spiritual journey of the author. The content within is not intended as medical, psychological, or legal advice, and it should not be interpreted as such. The use of Ayahuasca, as discussed in this book, is a highly individual and culturally specific practice. While some individuals may find transformative experiences, Ayahuasca is not universally effective or safe for all people. The use of Ayahuasca is subject to legal regulations and restrictions in many countries, including the United States, where it is classified as a controlled substance under federal law.

The author does not encourage or condone the illegal use of Ayahuasca or any other psychoactive substances. The experiences shared in this book are personal and anecdotal, and the author makes no claims regarding the health benefits or therapeutic outcomes of Ayahuasca. Readers are advised to exercise caution, seek professional advice, and comply with local laws and regulations regarding the use of plant medicines.

This book respects the cultural and spiritual traditions associated with Ayahuasca, particularly those of Indigenous communities in the Amazon. Any reference to these traditions is intended to honor their sacredness and significance. The author does not seek to appropriate or misrepresent the practices of these cultures.

By reading this book, you agree to take personal responsibility for your actions and decisions. The information provided is for educational and personal insight purposes only.

Prelude

The Sacred Dance of Shiva and Shakti

In Shiva's stillness, Shakti's sacred light,
Their union dances through eternal night.
When fear takes root within your mortal mind,
It weaves illusion of a denser kind.
Each thought of dread, a veil across pure space,
Obscuring truth's eternal, boundless face.

Within their dance all forms arise and fade,
Like waves upon an ocean, briefly made.
These shadows that your anxious mind conceives
Are ripples that the cosmic dancing weaves.
Yet peer beyond appearance' fleeting art,
To where all forms to formless light depart.

In that still point let Shakti's force ignite
With Shiva's gaze that sets all worlds aright,
Your fears dissolve like mist in morning sun
For seer and seen and seeing all are One.
In this eternal, ever-present grace,
No separate self remains to have a place.

Before pure Awareness made supreme,
All fears reveal themselves as but a dream.
For you are neither bound nor seeking free
You are the dance, the witness, and the sea.

This truth, when realized, leaves nothing more:
Just This, just Here, just Now, forevermore.

Prologue

I have always sensed a deeper meaning underlying life—something invisible that transcends the mundane rhythms and transient experiences encompassing our daily existence. An enigmatic veil disguises the true fabric of reality, revealing a boundless depth just beyond our grasp. The notion that we are born confined to the passage of time and then fade into nothingness strikes me as not only inadequate but also absurd. Life, with its intricate beauty and depth, cannot simply be a coincidental occurrence or a series of meaningless events. A purpose must exist—a reason, or at the very least, an understanding of our existence and our trajectory.

This relentless yearning, this subtle unrest, has planted within me a desire to comprehend what dwells beyond appearance. My pursuit of life's deeper meanings has been anything but straightforward. It has led me to exhilarating peaks of joy and wonder, only to drag me into the depths of despair and disillusionment. Yet, throughout this journey, my quest has remained unwavering, propelled by the firm belief that answers lie in wait, eager to be uncovered. This insatiable thirst for significance has become my guiding star, navigating me through the labyrinthine paths of life and urging me forward even when the way appears obscured.

Two decades ago, I came across a documentary that significantly altered the course of my life. It examined the fascinating interplay between Buddhism, consciousness, and modern physics—three domains that seem disparate yet, when intertwined, hint at profound realities regarding our existence. The concepts outlined in the documentary resonated deeply with me, igniting a response I had not previously felt. Buddhism, with its principles of the Middle Path, the Four Noble Truths, and the Eightfold Path, offered profound revelations about suffering, awareness, and the human experience. These ancient teachings contained the keys to inquiries I had quietly pondered throughout the years.

This invigorated curiosity propelled me into the realm of science, particularly Physics. While Buddhism provided a philosophical framework for understanding existence, my fascination with Physics encouraged me to seek empirical validation for those insights. My enthrallment with quantum mechanics, where subatomic particles engage in behavior that defies logic—existing in multiple states simultaneously and influencing each other across immense distances—unveiled a universe brimming with possibilities. Reality emerged not as the rigid, predictable entity I had assumed but instead as a dynamic, interconnected tapestry driven by probabilities.

In pursuit of this understanding, I devoted myself to academia, earning a Bachelor's degree in Physics, a Master's degree in Applied Physics, and a Ph.D. in Data Science. My doctoral research investigated the nexus of quantum computing, artificial intelligence, and medical diagnostics—a domain that connects the physical with the abstract. Yet, despite these academic achievements, the most profound inquiries concerning consciousness, the mysteries of the universe, and our existential purpose remained elusive. I had acquired the instruments to scrutinize the physical world but remained far from grasping the nature of reality or the mysteries that initially ignited my journey.

A serendipitous conversation with an old friend unexpectedly altered the course of my path. Although we hadn't spoken in years, our shared fascination with life's profound mysteries was swiftly reignited. As we reconnected, she introduced a topic I had never genuinely contemplated: psychedelics. She spoke of psilocybin mushrooms not as recreational drugs but as powerful instruments for self-exploration and spiritual enlightenment. She recounted how these experiences had led her to encounter a divine aspect of herself, a connection to the essence of existence. Her words piqued my interest, though I remained cautious. Could such substances really unlock insights that my years of study of Physics and Philosophy had failed to unveil?

The conversation left me with a blend of skepticism and curiosity. My scientific inclination demanded proof, leading me to delve into the works of renowned psychonauts like Terence and Dennis McKenna. Terence McKenna's explorations of altered states of awareness were compelling, particularly his suggestion of the "heroic dose" of seven grams of psilocybin mushrooms as a gateway to transformative experiences. He characterized this as a profound plunge into the mysteries of the mind and the universe, suited for the intrepid. His narratives of encountering alternate realities, ineffable truths, and the dissolution of self were both awe-inspiring and daunting.

Eventually, my curiosity triumphed. I decided to embark on this journey, carefully preparing my "set and setting" to ensure a safe and meaningful experience. I ingested the "heroic dose" of psilocybin mushrooms, enhanced with lemon juice to amplify their effects. What transpired was nothing short of extraordinary—an experience that completely redefined my understanding of reality.

The sound waves surrounded me, appearing as visible, palpable circles of energy that rippled through the room. The solidity of the physical realm began to dissipate; walls flowed like liquid, and objects pulsed with an underlying energy. The elementary particles I had long studied, renowned for their superposition and entanglement, liberated themselves from equations and laboratory settings. Reality unveiled quantum mechanics in action—not merely theoretical constructs but an immediate, visceral engagement with its fluid, interconnected essence.

The boundaries separating the external world from my inner consciousness disintegrated, exposing a state of profound unity. The fundamental nature of existence revealed itself, disclosing truths that transcended language and rationale. My years of textbook study, attending lectures, and conducting experiments diminished in comparison to this living encounter with a vibrant, dynamic, and infinitely complex experience. In those moments, the mysteries I sought transformed from intellectual pursuits into demands for firsthand experience. This venture into the unknown awakened a dormant aspect within me, marking a pivotal turning point that would forever influence my relationship with life, science, and the quest for meaning.

This evolved perspective soon unveiled an even deeper mystery: Ayahuasca, a revered brew cherished by the indigenous cultures of the Amazon. Distinct from any experience I had previously had, Ayahuasca combines two plants: *Banisteriopsis caapi* , a vine serving as the brew's spiritual anchor, and *Psychotria viridis* , a leaf containing the powerful psychoactive compound dimethyltryptamine (DMT). Together, these plants create a synergistic medicine that reveals the hidden layers of the mind and spirit. Ayahuasca transcends its physical manifestation as a brew to become a teacher, healer, guide, and bridge to realms of understanding far surpassing the ordinary.

For generations—potentially millennia—this ancient medicine has facilitated healing, divination, and connections to elevated awareness through Amazonian shamans. The shamans, known as curanderos and curanderas in South America, are deeply attuned to the jungle's rhythms and the spirits of plants. They guide seekers through the Ayahuasca journey, ensuring their safety and facilitating their healing. Their sacred songs, known as *icaros* , transform into conduits of energy rather than mere chants, weaving a bridge between the physical and spiritual realms. Through these songs, they channel the wisdom of plants, creating a space where participants confront their fears, release emotional burdens, and attain profound insights into their lives and the universe.

Ayahuasca stands among many ancient guides to the unseen. Across continents and epochs, civilizations have embraced similar tools to peer into the obscure. Hunter-gatherer societies in the Americas, Eurasia, Australia, and Africa wove psychoactive plants into their rituals, integrating them into their cultural and spiritual frameworks. These ceremonies transcended individual healing, evolving into collective experiences that bound communities in shared reverence for existential mysteries.

The Eleusinian Mysteries of ancient Greece encapsulated secret initiation rites. These seasonal ceremonies centered around *kykeon* , a psychoactive drink believed to contain ergot fungi rich in LSD-like alkaloids. Pilgrims engaging in these rites emerged profoundly transformed, sharing visions illuminating the essence of life and death. The Scythians of the Pontic Steppe incorporated cannabis into funeral rites—a practice documented by historian Herodotus and validated through archaeological findings. These rituals extended beyond symbolism, becoming bridges to the Divine and opening altered states of perception where the veil between the mortal and the eternal thinned.

The *Rigveda* , one of the oldest texts of Vedic literature, references *soma* , a sacred drink prized for its ability to connect humanity with the Divine. Although its precise formulation remains elusive, soma's significance as a psychoactive brew emphasizes the universality of this practice. The *Avesta* , Zoroastrian scripture, echoes this reverence by describing *hoama* , a drink that facilitates spiritual insight and communion with higher realms. The Mayan civilization incorporated psychoactive rituals into its complex societies, utilizing substances like psilocybin mushrooms to achieve altered states of awareness during religious ceremonies, thereby establishing connections with gods and the cosmos. These cultures recognized these plants as divine spirits that demanded respect, intention, and preparation. Their traditions, deeply woven into their cosmologies, unveiled the profound bond that connects the human spirit to the greater universe.

Preparing for the journey ahead connected me with these ancient practices. Ayahuasca is not an isolated occurrence but a testament to our species' persistent quest for understanding the meaning of life. This medicine, akin to *kykeon* , *soma* , *hoama* , or the sacred plants of the Maya, possesses the potential to unlock a portal to the essence of the human experience.

Ayahuasca transcends its role as merely a chemical catalyst for altered states; it emerges as a healer. The medicine delves deep into the human psyche, unearthing long-buried traumas and illuminating patterns that no longer serve us. Participants often describe their encounters as dialogues with a maternal, intelligent presence—"Mother Ayahuasca"—who leads them with both compassion and authority, unveiling truths that challenge yet ultimately transform. This medicine bypasses surface symptoms to tackle root causes, facilitating healing from within.

The sacred journey of Ayahuasca unveils pathways to profound emotional release, spiritual awakening, and a deep sense of unity with the universe. Under the guidance of a shaman, participants dive into the depths of their souls, healing ancient wounds while emerging with newfound clarity and purpose. The ancient brew catalyzes transformation not through simplistic answers but by illuminating the truths residing within.

Ayahuasca symbolizes a sacred key, unlocking realms far beyond ordinary perception. For centuries, cultures worldwide have embraced psychoactive substances as instruments to explore these hidden dimensions of existence. These Earth-given gifts serve not only as agents of healing but also as bridges to divine communion, self-discovery, and the search for significance in our vast, mysterious cosmos. Among these ancient practices, Ayahuasca's unparalleled capacity to reveal the layers of human consciousness marks it as an ineffably transformative medicine.

For participants embarking on this sacred journey, Ayahuasca discloses profound emotional release, spiritual awakening, and deep interconnectedness with the universe. With the careful guidance of shamans, seekers explore the depths of their souls, heal old wounds, and emerge transformed. This ancient brew holds the promise of change not through facile solutions but by unveiling the truths that reside within.

After a year of exploration, I felt drawn to Spirit Quest Sanctuary. Founded by the renowned Chavín maestro, Don Howard Lawler, Spirit Quest transcends conventional retreat experiences, evolving into a sacred haven where physical and spiritual realms converge, inviting seekers to delve into the depths of consciousness. Nestled near Iquitos, Peru, the sanctuary rests within the heart of the Peruvian Amazon—a region celebrated for its extraordinary biodiversity and mystical allure.

Spanning 150 hectares of unspoiled rainforest, the sanctuary creates an immersive setting in which nature serves as an educator. Majestic ceiba trees, known as the "trees of life," stand watch over the landscape, their roots anchoring the sanctuary while their branches reach skyward in eternal homage. The vibrant jungle pulses with life; the calls of birds, the distant howls of monkeys, and the rustling of unseen wildlife combine to form a wild symphony that resonates with the rhythms of the soul.

Winding paths weave seamlessly into the environment, guiding visitors through this expansive landscape. The forest breathes with ancient wisdom, whispering secrets to those willing to listen. Small, traditional wooden rooms are scattered throughout the sanctuary, offering guests simple yet comfortable accommodations that strike a balance between solitude and connection to nature. Crafted from eco-friendly materials, these rooms invite visitors in with hammocks and mosquito nets, immersing them in the sights and sounds of the jungle.

Two ceremonial *malocas* , circular structures built with traditional materials, anchor the sanctuary's core. These sacred spaces form the spiritual epicenter of the retreat, where participants gather for ceremonies of Ayahuasca and Huachuma, also known as the San Pedro cactus. The malocas, architectural wonders open to the elements yet sheltered by palm-thatched roofs, integrate the surrounding jungle into the healing experience. Candlelight flickers within, creating an atmosphere of reverence and illuminating the faces of those seeking answers, healing, or transformation.

Don Howard's teachings, rooted in the ancient Chavín tradition, imbue every aspect of Spirit Quest with purpose and intention. He revealed Mother Ayahuasca to be a living intelligence, an ancient spirit imparting profound wisdom to those prepared to undertake the challenging inner work that it necessitates. His legacy endures through his daughter, Selva Lawler, whose compassionate guidance and deep understanding continue to uphold the sanctuary's mission.

The Spirit Quest Sanctuary transcends mere physical space to become an experiential odyssey—a journey into the heart of the Amazon and the depths of the soul. The convergence of forest, medicine, and teachings creates an environment where transformation unfolds organically and inevitably. This sanctuary melds the mystical beauty of the natural world into both a setting and stimulus for profound healing and self-discovery.

My journey into this profound exploration of self unfolded in a nonlinear fashion. My initial application to Spirit Quest Sanctuary filled me with anticipation, as I was eager to advance in my quest for answers. However, life charted a different course. Unforeseen hurdles arose, and despite my fervent desire to connect with Mother Ayahuasca's wisdom, I could not attend. The perceived obstacles in my way held a hidden purpose, slowly revealing themselves as part of a grander design. The timing awaited perfection; I required preparation for the transformative depths that Spirit Quest Sanctuary would provide.

Two transformative retreats at Nimea Kaya Sanctuary, deep in the Amazon rainforest near Pucallpa, amplified Mother Ayahuasca's call with resonant clarity. Nimea Kaya birthed my journey with Mother Ayahuasca; her sacred energy and jungle connection awakened dormant depths within me. The lush surroundings pulsed with the natural concerto of the rainforest, drawing me into a more profound exploration of both the external world and the uncharted territories of my soul.

Following these life-altering retreats, a new chapter unfolded. This ongoing guidance led me to Spirit Quest Sanctuary, where yet another layer of transformation awaited. The sanctity of the land exuded a familiar power coupled with a distinct character, inviting me further along my spiritual journey and deepening the insights I had gained at Nimea Kaya. Spirit Quest welcomed me, promising new lessons, healing, and a refined understanding of the mysteries I had just begun to unveil.

Thus, my journey began.

At the heart of Nimea Kaya Sanctuary are the Shipibo curanderos and curanderas, master healers whose ancestral knowledge of plant medicine spans generations. Their profound connection with Ayahuasca and the spirit realm infuses every *icaro* they sing during ceremonies. These songs evolve into energetic maps, guiding participants through their inner landscapes and serving as lifelines during the challenging yet transformative healing process. The shamans' guidance initiated me into an unparalleled journey of discovery.

The ceremonies revealed deep humility alongside profound illumination, taking me into realms that no level of preparation could fully anticipate. The sacred space of the maloca enveloped me in quiet surrender to the unknown. Energy coursed through the maloca, making it an active participant in our unfolding journey. The shamans' sacred *icaros* filled the air with ancient wisdom, establishing a foundation for my transformative encounter with Mother Ayahuasca.

Mother Ayahuasca acted both as a teacher and a mirror, reflecting hidden dimensions of myself—fears, regrets, and traumas I had buried so deeply that I had convinced myself they no longer existed. Yet they lingered in the shadows of my psyche, influencing my decisions, relationships, and self-perception without my conscious awareness. Mother Ayahuasca brought them to light with steadfast clarity, illuminating aspects of myself I had long eluded or ignored.

Initially, this confrontation proved unsettling. The intensity of the visions and emotions overwhelmed me as layers of my mind peeled back one by one. Vivid imagery materialized: scenes from my past, forgotten memories, and symbolic representations of my inner conflicts. I recognized the faces of those I had wronged and those who had wronged me, feeling the weight of unresolved grief, anger, and shame in real-time. Mother Ayahuasca refused to let me avert my gaze; it demanded my complete focus, compelling me to confront the discomfort and acknowledge the truths I had been reluctant to face. Yet intertwined with this unflinching honesty was undeniable compassion.

Mother Ayahuasca gently guided me through, conveying that while the journey entailed pain, it was crucial for healing. The medicine revealed these shadows not as adversaries but as parts of myself yearning for recognition and integration. They emerged as wounds longing for acknowledgment, not to harm me but to help me understand the deeper patterns of my life.

As I allowed myself to confront these emotions fully —grieving past losses, seeking forgiveness for myself and others, and releasing the weight of unexpressed truths—I felt a tremendous sense of relief. The heavy burden I had borne for years dissipated. The maloca became a sacred container for this release, its walls resonating with the shamans' *icaros* , guiding me through the tempest of my emotions with expert precision.

By the end of the ceremonies, I felt an overwhelming sense of gratitude. Mother Ayahuasca unveiled that authentic healing begins with the courage to confront oneself wholly and earnestly. Through this process, I came to understand that my fears and regrets were not obstacles to my growth but stepping stones toward wholeness. The shadows I had grappled with became integral pieces of the puzzle that shaped my identity. Through this humbling and enlightening journey, I rediscovered a more authentic connection with myself, with others, and with the breathtaking tapestry of existence.

This journey stripped away layers of pretense and self-preservation I had constructed over the years, leaving me raw and exposed to my emotions. The experience was visceral, relentless, and profoundly emotional—a reckoning with myself that I could neither evade nor escape. The intensity grew overwhelming as waves of sorrow, anger, fear, and shame surged through me. I was deconstructed piece by piece, with every repressed memory and buried trauma surfacing, demanding my full attention.

Amidst this emotional tempest, purpose emerged. The discomfort bore significance and necessity. Mother Ayahuasca functioned as a soul surgeon, excising the unhealthy elements of my psyche to reveal an unstained core beneath. Each painful realization and unspoken truth contributed to a more extensive process of release and renewal. The grip of old wounds eased, their sharpness lessening as I allowed myself to fully embrace and subsequently relinquish the emotions I had long evaded. These moments surpassed mere catharsis; they became profound acts of liberation, each one freeing me from a weight I had carried for years.

The medicine operated with ancient wisdom, knowing precisely what I needed to confront and when. As the pain oscillated, moments of profound clarity emerged—glimpses of truths transcending language or intellect. These insights manifested as direct, undeniable experiences arising from the very fabric of existence.

I glimpsed the interconnectedness of all things—the intricate web of life intertwining us in ways that surpass understanding. I experienced an overwhelming love—not the fleeting, conditional affection often encountered, but a boundless, universal love encompassing everything and everyone, including myself. In those profound moments, I tapped into consciousness, an infinite source of awareness and comprehension that had long awaited my awakening.

These flashes of connection and clarity pierced through the darkness like a lighthouse, illuminating the path ahead. They offered me a refreshed perspective on my pain and past, interpreting these experiences as elements of a larger narrative—a journey of growth, healing, and transformation. Mother Ayahuasca did not erase my hardships or provide straightforward resolutions; instead, it bestowed upon me the tools to comprehend and integrate them, framing them as vital aspects of my life's mosaic.

In place of anguish blossomed a newfound peace and wholeness. This tranquility emerged not from evading discomfort but from embracing it, recognizing that I had confronted my shadows and emerged more resilient. The experience transformed me entirely, guiding me through the depths of my being and leaving me with a greater understanding of myself, my place in the world, and the boundless nature of existence.

Through these experiences, I internalized that genuine healing does not imply erasing the past, pretending it never happened, or burying it deeper within the recesses of the mind. Healing transforms our relationship with the past, altering how we bear it, perceive it, and how it shapes our present and future. Mother Ayahuasca did not magically erase my pain or rewrite my history; instead, it provided clarity, enabling me to see my experiences through a new lens. The medicine offered a perspective that encouraged me to view my life with profound compassion and understanding, illuminating the lessons cloaked within even the most painful memories.

The journey empowered me. Mother Ayahuasca taught me how to heal myself rather than simply providing healing. It unveiled the patterns in my life that had previously escaped my notice—the unconscious habits and beliefs that kept me ensnared in cycles of pain or limitation. It revealed the threads connecting my choices, relationships, and self-identity, allowing me to untangle them with newfound awareness. With each ceremony, I discovered that the power to change, evolve, and heal had always existed within me, awaiting acknowledgment and activation.

This transformation blossomed not only through the medicine but also through the environment itself. Nimea Kaya emerged as more than just a retreat; it became a sanctuary for transformation—a sacred space within which the physical and spiritual realms converged. The vibrant energy of the Amazon rainforest enveloped me, amplifying the medicine's teachings and wisdom. The ambient sounds of the forest—the chirping insects, rustling leaves, and distant wildlife calls—provided a harmonious backdrop for introspection and connection. Each facet of the retreat, from the ceremonial maloca to the caregivers' nurturing presence, affirmed and supported this profound work.

Within this sanctuary, I discovered the power of surrender. The medicine compelled me to relinquish control, trust the process, and allow emotions to flow freely. Embracing surrender proved challenging, requiring me to confront the unknown, dwell in discomfort, and permit feelings to surface unimpeded. By surrendering, I unearthed remarkable resilience within myself—a strength I had not previously recognized. By submitting to the process, I emerged renewed and awakened.

The transformation pervaded my being, extending beyond the internal to manifest holistically. My body and spirit felt lighter, liberated from years of accumulated burdens. My connection to the world deepened, revealing the interdependence of all things—not merely as a concept to be understood but as a lived reality. My healing contributed to a grander narrative, where threads intertwine through shared experiences, emotions, and energies.

Nimea Kaya and Spirit Quest Sanctuaries provided more than mere healing; they gifted me with a new way of existing—a fresh perspective from which to view the world with open eyes and a receptive heart. In these sacred spaces, I laid aside the burdens of my past and embraced a more authentic version of myself, guided by Mother Ayahuasca's wisdom and the Amazon's sanctity. This began my lifelong voyage of growth, connection, and transformation.

My path forward unveiled itself not merely as a quest for answers but as an inviting embrace into the mystery with open hands and an open heart. Mother Ayahuasca demanded surrender, releasing preconceived notions and the grip of the ego. In return, it promised clarity, healing, and a connection to a far greater reality than the individual self. The medicine showed who I was, who I had been, and who I will eternally remain. This journey offered no shortcuts but served as a sacred tool—a mirror highlighting truths that transcended ordinary perception.

As I readied myself for the upcoming trip, anticipation intertwined with anxiety. This journey demanded monumental responsibility, requiring the preparation of body, mind, and spirit. The path extended beyond seeking answers to discovering the questions that genuinely held significance.

Ayahuasca, akin to the ancient rites of the Greeks, the Scythians, and the Vedic sages, opened a portal to eternity. Stepping through promised not just an encounter with the unknown but also the unveiling of the Absolute. As I stood on the threshold, I sensed my readiness—not solely to search but to become.

Chapter One

The Great Cleansing

The first encounter with Mother Ayahuasca took place at Nimea Kaya, a sacred sanctuary nestled in the vibrant heart of Pucallpa, Peru. The evening air, rich with earthy fragrances, carried the whispers of the jungle as the sun dipped below the horizon, yielding its golden rays to the coming night. The rainforest around us seemed alive with unseen energies, as if the spirits of the land were waking to accompany us on our journey. Small traditional wooden huts, named *tambos* , scattered throughout the sanctuary offered simple yet comfortable accommodations, striking the perfect balance between solitude and connection to nature.

The tambos, nestled amid the jungle, immersed seekers in the sights and sounds of the wild, allowing them to rest in harmony with the surrounding environment. At the center of it all stood the ceremonial maloca, an open and sacred space that held the deepest reverence for the ceremonies performed within. Its palm-thatched roof offered shelter from the elements while connecting us to the earth below. Inside, flickering candlelight danced across the wooden beams, setting the atmosphere for the spiritual journey ahead. The maloca, with its ancient energy, became a vessel for transformation, where the wisdom of the shamans, combined with the profound energy of the jungle, guided us into the sacred realms of healing.

At 6:00 p.m., a shamanic duo—a man and a woman—entered the maloca. Their serene yet commanding presence altered the atmosphere with quiet elegance. The ceremonial roundhouse flickered with the glow of candles, casting playful shadows on the walls. The air was charged with expectation as if the jungle paused in silent acknowledgment of the profound transformation about to unfold.

Unlike the other participants who arrived just before the ceremony began, I had the rare opportunity to witness the sacred preparations early on. This privilege resonated deeply with me. I settled into silence, observing as the shamans performed their rituals with intentional, deliberate gestures. Their communication flowed silently through gestures and subtle glances; their connection to the space and each other was palpable in the air.

The shamans began cleansing the maloca with *mapacho* , sacred tobacco smoke that flowed gracefully through the air, accompanied by small bottles of *agua florida* , a spiritually charged fragrant water. The rich, earthy scent of tobacco mingled with the citrusy sweetness of the agua florida, creating an atmosphere both grounding and ethereal. Each exhaled cloud of smoke and whispered prayer enveloped the space in invisible protection, safeguarding it against any malevolent energies.

Their icaros passed down through generations, emerged softly like whispers before crescendoing with power and rhythm. These songs transcended melody, becoming vibrant conduits of sacred energy that reverberated in the air. The sound resonated deep within me, reviving something ancient and eternal. The maloca transformed, enveloped in a cocoon of light and intention—a sanctuary for healing and rebirth, untouched by negative influences.

Humbled, I sat quietly on my mat, closing my eyes to immerse myself in the energy around me. Each chant and the gentle rustle of the chakapa leaves breathed vitality into the maloca. The structure morphed into a living organism, pulsating in sync with the jungle, its heartbeat harmonizing with the shamans' songs. Their fleeting glances radiated warmth and understanding as my energy blended seamlessly into their sacred tapestry, balancing masculine and feminine forces to cultivate harmony within the maloca.

As the final protective layers settled, an enveloping stillness blanketed the space. The maloca became a universe, a realm where time and space surrendered to the soulful journey ahead. The sounds of the jungle softened in deference while the steady flicker of candlelight cast a warm, golden illumination.

With their work nearly complete, the shamans halted, exchanging grateful nods. Their glance communicated quiet appreciation for my role in this sacred creation. A sense of belonging and purpose swelled in my heart, an acknowledgment of the rarity of this moment.

Other participants arrived, stepping cautiously into the transformed maloca. They moved with hesitation, their faces marked by nervous expectation and reverence, unaware of the meticulous preparations that had taken place in their absence. From my vantage point, I watched them settle in as the shamans greeted each individual with a calm, steady presence, their earlier work setting the tone for our upcoming ceremony.

By 8:00 p.m., the ceremony commenced. A deep connection enveloped me, intertwining the space, the shamans, and the purpose of the evening. The maloca was no longer just a structure in the jungle; it had transformed into a sacred temple, a vessel for metamorphosis imbued with ancient wisdom and divine energy. A palpable vibe flowed through the atmosphere, alive and ready to guide us into the depths of our souls.

One of the facilitators brought us the cup with the medicine after the bottle of Ayahuasca had been blessed once more by the shamans. The dark, viscous liquid caught and reflected the flickering candlelight as we remained on our mats, each of us preparing for the journey ahead. The potent aroma of the brew—a blend of rich earthiness—reached me before the cup touched my lips—a living infusion of soil, roots, and something beyond description. Taking a grounding breath, I tilted the cup back, allowing the thick, bitter liquid to flow into my mouth.

The sharp medicinal taste clung to the back of my throat. I fought the urge to wince and swallowed, knowing this transient discomfort would precede a profound journey. Once the last drop slipped away, I returned the cup and sank onto my mat, enveloped by the sacred energy of the maloca.

The shamans' icaros soared, intertwining with the heartbeat of the jungle. Although sung in a tongue unfamiliar to me, the songs stirred ancient echoes within. The spirits of the rainforest seemed to harmonize with their voices, each note gently steering me toward the unknown. Our small circle of six, along with several facilitators, sat quietly, wrapped in a shroud of apprehension. I covered my eyes with a sleep mask, cutting myself off from the outer world.

Time began to unravel. Thirty minutes may have passed, perhaps more or less—measurement lost its significance. Time's firm grip loosened as ambient sounds from the jungle washed over me. The symphony of crickets, the calls of night birds, and the rustle of leaves formed a hypnotic melody that echoed within and around me.

With my eyes closed, I anchored myself in the steady rhythm of my breath amid growing anticipation. A question took root in my thoughts, repeating like a whispered prayer: "Mother Ayahuasca, are you here?" Each utterance carried sacred intent, charged with longing and humility. Beyond my quest for presence, I surrendered myself entirely to her revelations.

The question soared, echoing through my mind like whispers carried by the wind—subtle yet insistent. "Mother Ayahuasca, are you here?" These words traversed an unseen expanse, bridging my conscious awareness with her enigmatic realm. My heart, pounding in anticipation, punctuated the serene stillness.

The jungle responded. Leaves rustled louder, their whispers nearing comprehension as the earth began to stir. Shamanic icaros wove through the air, threading the maloca with sacred energy. Their resonant voices coursed through me, igniting profound inner knowing.

Yet, I remained still, repeating, "Mother Ayahuasca, are you here?" The mantra transcended mere words, transforming into an earnest offering, a supplication, and a release. Each repetition deepened my vulnerability and willingness to remain open to her infinite wisdom.

The charged air vibrated with uncertainty. This stillness brimmed with fullness, pulsating with presence just beyond my reach. My breath slowed as I surrendered completely, and the question echoed one last time through the vast landscape of my consciousness.

A gentle yet unmistakable shift rippled through the stillness—a slight stirring in the depths of my awareness. The maloca reverberated with quiet intensity, anticipating her arrival. My heart quickened as I sensed the journey beginning.

Just as doubt threatened to engulf my faith, a voice emerged from the depths of silence. It was not heard through my ears but resonated within me, speaking with gentle firmness and undeniable authority. The voice carried both love and discipline, resembling a wise elder who sees through the layers of pretense to reveal unfiltered truth.

Words broke through the mental fog: "If you don't stop asking foolish questions, I'll have to set you straight! Can't you understand I'm busy cleaning up the mess you've made of yourself?" Sharp yet humorous, the remark jolted me from my spiraling thoughts. It was neither cruel nor coddling—exactly what I needed.

The voice embodied the unconditional love of a grandmother melded with unwavering accountability. It recognized me, flaws and all while clarifying my missteps. Those few words conveyed profound care paired with a clear acknowledgment of the work ahead. No judgment tainted her tone, only an unvarnished recognition of my internal discord.

Her undeniable presence rendered me speechless. She had observed me quietly all along, poised for the right moment to speak. Her voice flowed like pure energy, shaking loose, deeply rooted doubts and fears. I grasped her profound lesson. My persistent question, "Are you here?" now felt trivial, almost laughable. She had always been present, and my inquiry merely highlighted my resistance to the process.

Her words carried profound depth beyond their surface meaning. They reminded me of my purpose there: the inner purification demanded by Mother Ayahuasca. This journey called for surrender, not for seeking comfort. Her reply invited trust and the relinquishment of control, allowing for a natural unfolding. An internal change occurred; self-doubt and impatience evaporated, replaced by humility and acceptance. I was there to listen, learn, and follow Mother Ayahuasca's guidance along her immaculate path.

I lifted my mask, my breath shallow with curiosity and trepidation as the dim candlelight of the maloca flickered around me. My eyes struggled to adjust, drawn to a narrow ray of light slicing through the shadows. Instinctively, I inspected my hands, my only tether to the familiar; what I beheld defied comprehension. My hands, the extensions of my physical being, began to morph and shift before my eyes. Initially subtle—a faint distortion akin to heat rippling over a desert road. But as the transformation unfolded, it deepened.

My body began its return to the earth with serene grace. Patches of deep purple and jade appeared across my skin like watercolor strokes, radiating outward from my center in gentle waves. My flesh softened and sank, pulling away from my bones in a silent surrender. The familiar contours of my form transformed as internal spaces rearranged, my skin thinning like parchment. The metamorphosis advanced—skin melted into the air like morning mist, unveiling layers of amber-hued tissue beneath. Muscles unwound like fragile threads, and bones began to emerge like pale moonlight. Tendons and ligaments loosened their grasp, allowing joints to drift apart in a slow, graceful dance of dissolution. I was witnessing the gradual return of my form to its elemental state, unraveling into simplicity until the distinction between self and earth became a striking blend.

The final phase of my dissolution flowed like water dissolving into sand. My remaining essence merged with the earth, not as decay but as pure energy returning to its origin. As the last remnants of my physical self fused with the soil, the landscape began to vanish. This was not destruction but a realm of pure potential—a blank canvas glowing with possibility. Every trace of past experiences and accumulated karma evaporated into nothingness. The land lay stripped and immaculate, reset to its primordial state, poised for the first whisper of creation.

This experience was both unsettling and exhilarating. The boundaries that had defined me—my body, my identity, my sense of separateness—were dissolving into a boundless ocean of existence. I wasn't disappearing; I was expanding. Each moment drew me closer to something ancient and infinite, pulsating with the essence of life itself.

Suddenly, overwhelming clarity struck. This wasn't a mere vision but a revelation. The disintegration of my physical form mirrored a profound truth: the self I had clung to was an illusion, a mask worn in the grand performance of existence. Stripped of this mask, I wasn't nothing; I was everything. I was the space between stars, the breath of the jungle, the quiet hum of the universe itself.

This dissolution wasn't an end but a beginning. It was a return to my true essence, a state beyond form and limitation. I was not merely shedding layers; I was entering a new kind of existence, transcending the confines of my physical realm. In that expanse of boundless awareness, a profound peace enveloped me as if I had finally come home to my true self.

My inner vision expanded to a vast white screen arising from the void, stretching infinitely into the enclosing darkness. A cinematic reel began to play, flickering to life with a clarity and richness that felt more real than any waking memory. The film raced backward with astonishing velocity, carrying me along a vortex of moments interwoven with personal and universal significance.

Scenes from my life unfolded in reverse, each frame more vivid than the last. I witnessed the carefree days of childhood, pivotal milestones that shaped me, and even the seemingly insignificant moments long forgotten. Every fragment of memory unraveled, peeling away layers of my existence. This was not just a review of my life; life itself unraveled in a way that illuminated the interconnectedness of every experience.

The reel went further back, penetrating the veil of this life to unveil the mysteries of others. I was propelled beyond the confines of my current identity into long-forgotten lifetimes. Faces I didn't recognize yet instinctively knew appeared—companions, adversaries, and loved ones from ages past. Entire worlds, both familiar and alien, flashed by in an instant, each holding fragments of lost truths.

Events from these lives unfolded, their significance profound yet just out of reach. I witnessed myself in roles I had never imagined: sometimes a leader, sometimes a wanderer, and sometimes a mere bystander. The emotions tied to these moments surged within me—triumph, heartbreak, joy, and regret—interwoven into the intricate fabric of my soul's journey.

The reel moved with such speed that time itself faded away. The divisions between lives dissolved, leaving only the essence of existence—a continuous flow of experiences, lessons, and transformations. Each lifetime formed a thread in an infinite tapestry, and I understood that these threads were not distinct but part of a greater whole.

As the images continued to unfold, a sense of familiarity intensified. I inhabited these lives entirely, feeling their weight and significance within my being. They were not distant echoes; they were part of me. The choices, struggles, and triumphs of each life contributed to this moment—the moment of sitting in the maloca, guided by Mother Ayahuasca.

The reel slowed. Images faded, the screen dissolved, and I hovered in profound stillness, suspended in the void. In that silence, a realization struck with undeniable force: my identity transcended this body, this mind, this life. I embodied the culmination of countless journeys, each contributing to the infinite essence of who I truly am, as both the actor and the witness, the dreamer and the dream, eternally intertwined in the cosmic flow of existence.

Then, the truth emerged—not as a thought, but as an overwhelming presence: I had died, though it was a different kind of death. It was a departure from this life, an exit from the constraints of the body and mind into a boundless state of awareness. Yet instead of fear or sorrow, profound serenity enveloped me—an acceptance so deep that it dissolved every trace of resistance. The burdens of life—the struggles, regrets, and relentless striving— evaporated. Each shackle binding me shattered, leaving behind an unfathomable lightness.

This was not a loss but a return—a return to something fundamental, eternal, lying quietly beneath the surface of existence. Where identity once resided, only pure awareness remained. No labels or roles could define me. The vastness cradled me, infinite and alive. The boundaries that had once defined me—my name, my body, my history—melted into the endless expanse of being.

This experience brought profound liberation. I stepped out of the heavy, ill-fitting garment of identity into an existence that felt effortless and natural. There was no past to regret, no future to fret about—only the eternal now, vibrant and pulsating with unspeakable joy.

In that state, I relinquished everything I believed I needed. There was no longing, no yearning, and no sense of incompleteness. I sought neither answers nor meaning, for I had become the answer and embodied the meaning. Beyond the absence of pain or struggle lay something extraordinary: an unshakeable wholeness that filled every aspect of my being.

At the core of this revelation, the true nature of death unveiled itself: not the finality I had dreaded but a radiant threshold shimmering with potential. Death shed its dark veils, revealing itself as a sacred passage between worlds, a conduit through which consciousness flows unbound. This was not the cold emptiness I had once contemplated but a vast expansion, like a drop of water merging with the ocean while retaining the memory of its journey as rain. Boundaries disintegrated, revealing an eternal now where the past and future became pure awareness.

Space transformed from a rigid container into a fluid dance of infinite possibility. The heaviness of corporeal form yielded a lighter, more meaningful existence that transcended shape and boundary. My soul, liberated from earthly constraints, unfurled like a flower opening to boundless light. This liberation brought neither annihilation of self nor preservation of ego but a profound remembering of my essence: consciousness witnessing itself in an endless array of forms, playing through countless expressions of being where existence required no justification or purpose; it simply was complete and perfect in its infinite unfolding.

As I sank deeper into this state of pure being, the barren earth beneath me sprang to life. A gentle tremor rippled through the dark soil, and life erupted in cascading waves of vibrant transformation. Delicate shoots of grass emerged from the soil, transforming into vibrant green blankets that danced gently in the soft wind. The verdant carpet spread like paint across a canvas, each blade catching light that seemed to emanate from within. Blossoms burst forth in a riot of color: crimson poppies bobbing on delicate stems, elegant violet lupines reaching skyward, and marigolds blazing like drops of molten sun. Each bloom emitted an intensity transcending ordinary perception, their colors so pure and vivid they appeared to radiate an internal glow. This magnificent transformation flowed like music made visible, nature's symphony orchestrating a sacred reminder of life's eternal rhythm.

From this flourishing oasis, sacred serpents emerged, embodying living dreams taking shape. Their sleek, powerful bodies wove through the flowers with mesmerizing grace. Each serpent moved with a distinct rhythm: some gliding swiftly, others undulating gently like waves upon ancient shores. Their scales formed intricate patterns that danced with each motion, capturing light in ways that defied reality. Emerald green deepened into forest shadows, brightening into spring leaf brilliance. Sapphire blue swirled with accents of turquoise and azure while golden glimmers danced across their forms like sunlight on pristine water. Some adorned themselves with diamond-shaped markings that pulsed with inner fire, while others exhibited spiral patterns that drew the eye into infinite depths. They possessed regal poise, exuding not only wisdom but the fundamental essence of knowledge, as if they had witnessed the birth of stars and held the secrets of creation in their silent stares. When they approached, the air thickened with their power, yet their presence evoked recognition, like encountering a long-forgotten truth.

The serpents moved toward me, around me, and eventually through me as though I was as permeable as the air itself. Their energy flowed as an extension of my being. They carried a sense of unity, a reminder that the perceived separateness between us was an illusion. There was no "me" and "them"; only Oneness prevailed.

When I peered down, my form had transformed. My skin mirrored their shimmering scales, a mosaic of greens and blues glinting like polished jewels. I belonged among them; I existed as one of them. Their essence coursed through me, merging with mine in a uniquely profound way. I felt no fear, only an overwhelming sense of belonging, as though I had rediscovered a part of myself that had long been hidden. I was life itself, dynamic and ever-evolving. The serpents embodied transformation, shedding their skins and stepping into a more authentic, deeply connected self. Their presence whispered truths that transcended language: life flows in cycles, change embraces sacred power, and by surrendering, I achieved wholeness.

A surge of nausea enveloped me, tightening its grip on my entire being. As I began to expel the contents of my stomach, I stumbled upon something primal and shadowy, long concealed in the farthest corners of my spirit. Each retch ignited a force within me, and with every heave, layers of darkness shed. Translucent serpents, once unblemished yet now corrupted, slithered from my mouth, writhing as they fell into the purging bucket.

The snakes bore more than just physical toxins; they carried the heavy burdens of pain, trauma, and memories etched into my very essence over many lifetimes. Peering into the bucket revealed fragments of an ancient and elemental nature intertwined with my existence. I had tapped into the core of my lineage, confronting the scars embedded in my DNA—unresolved battles, sorrows, and inherited weights passed down through generations.

The act of releasing fragmented not only my chains but also those of my ancestors. The purging transcended mere physicality, transforming into a sacred ritual of freedom and a reclamation of the purity of my soul. As the final remnants departed, I experienced an undeniable lightness and a profound sense of renewal. The energy I had expelled no longer held dominion over me.

When the purging at last ceased, a deep tranquility enveloped me, filling my spirit with an ethereal calm. An immense, oppressive burden—one I had scarcely recognized—lifted from the depths of my being. The release shattered unseen bonds forged across lifetimes, liberating me from long-held weights I had borne unknowingly.

My entire essence exhaled in relief, a resonant sigh echoing within me. I set free an age-old tension, tightly coiled and often concealed, unspooling in a single transformative moment. Everything around me shifted. The air turned crisp and electric, charged with life and rejuvenation. Each breath beckoned me to embrace this newfound liberation.

A revitalizing energy coursed through me, my cells rejoicing in their newfound freedom. My body felt weightless, my mind clearer, and my spirit unshackled. I had been granted a second chance to navigate life without encumbrance. The sounds of the surrounding jungle—the rustling leaves, the buzzing insects—echoed with a vibrant cadence that mirrored my internal renaissance. I existed entirely in the present, awake to the miracle of being.

The shamans' icaros drifted through the maloca, their songs forming a tender, restorative chrysalis of healing energy. The sound, gentle and pure, wove through the air, surrounding me as a palpable energy, embracing my mind and body. Every note resonated with the universe's wisdom, intricately designed to heal and unveil. The melodies reached me like living strands, linking me to something vaster than myself, transcending the limits of the physical realm.

The vibrations of their songs resonated within my innermost self, reaching the core of my essence. The music penetrated my bones, touching places where words could never reach. The icaros closed invisible wounds, mending fractures in my spirit and repairing the parts of me that past experiences had shattered. The surroundings opened, and I floated in a sea of sound, weightless and free, buoyed by the soothing rhythms of the shamans' voices.

As the shamans continued to sing, their icaros formed a protective shield of energy around me, like a comforting blanket. This warmth radiated tenderly, gently cradling my spirit and providing a sense of safety I had always yearned for but had never truly known. A profound emotional warmth seeped into my heart, dissolving the fears and anxieties I had carried. Each note of the icaros washed over me like a gentle tide, soothing the raw and exposed segments of my soul and filling them with healing light.

Every note served as a salve, tending to the fresh wounds left by my purging experience. Where pain once prevailed, serenity now occupied that space. Where tension once held sway, ease now flowed. The icaros not only soothed lingering emotional scars but also healed the energetic imprints of countless lifetimes of suffering. With every vibration, my essence softened, and I realized that healing could unfold delicately, like blooming petals in the light.

The sound of the icaros extended beyond the walls of the maloca, reaching into the very fabric of the universe. The shamans' voices harmonized in perfect unison, crafting a sacred resonance that unified all things—past, present, and future. The music echoed with an ancient familiarity, reverberating through the expansive corridors of existence. Each melody unlocked hidden realms of consciousness, inviting me to traverse them.

As I listened, a presence far grander than the shamans or the ceremony held me. The icaros became a bridge to the Divine, a holly dialect that spoke to my soul in ways words could never convey. I synchronized with the rhythm of the cosmos, becoming part of a grand orchestral masterpiece. The boundaries of my body dissipated, transforming me from an isolated entity into an integral component of everything—the stars, the trees, the earth, the air. Each cell within me vibrated in harmony with the cosmos' song.

I reclined on my mat, feeling the reassuring weight of the earth beneath me, grounding me to something that transcended the physical. My body merged with the floor, dissolving into the fabric of the earth. This sensation brought profound solace—the earth embraced me, fostering a deep connection and sense of belonging. The persistent noise of my thoughts, often preoccupied with mundane distractions, faded into silence, unveiling a remarkable stillness. My thoughts evaporated, revealing that they were never truly mine. In that moment, the past and future dissolved into the tranquil clarity of the present.

As I sank deeper into the mat, a wave of tranquility enveloped me. Not a fleeting calm but a profound, all-encompassing peace that permeated every fiber of my being. The air vibrated with serenity, and the universe aligned in perfect harmony. There was no effort, no striving—only existence. My breath flowed effortlessly, each inhalation and exhalation forming a natural cadence, while my heart beat steadily, anchoring me deeper into the moment. I relinquished control, residing in a space where surrendering to peace became the ultimate truth.

Gradually, my consciousness drifted away from the physical sensations, submerging into a deep, dreamless slumber. This was no ordinary rest; it reconnected me with the very source of existence itself, reawakening the primal, divine energy from which all life springs. I returned to the sacred womb, that sanctuary of safety, warmth, and endless potential. The gentle pulse of life surrounded me, echoing like a cosmic heartbeat, ensuring my safety and protection. The world beyond the maloca, the jungle, and the sounds of the ceremony faded into a distant hum, leaving only this cocoon of pure, untainted rest.

Something greater than myself engulfed me—a nurturing energy cradled me in absolute safety. Beyond the absence of fear, an overwhelming sense of unconditional love wrapped around me like a warm, glowing mantle. The universe's arms held me while the love and care of the cosmos flowed into my being. An innate understanding blossomed in my heart, assuring me that I was not alone; I was deeply loved and precisely where I was meant to be. This profound sense of being loved transcended any earthly limitations. The universe whispered that all was well—that I rested right where I needed to be: fully supported, fully loved, and ultimately, truly home.

Morning arrived, heralding the earth's awakening from a profound, peaceful slumber. Golden sunlight streamed through the gaps in the maloca's wooden walls, casting delicate rays of light across the sacred space. Each sunray breathed life into the room, filling the air with quiet, ethereal energy. The sunlight illuminated every detail, making the wooden beams and natural textures of the maloca radiate with divine brilliance. The atmosphere throbbed with the vibrancy of the new day.

The brightening light unveiled softly drifting specks of dust in the air, caught in the sunlight like tiny, glimmering stars. The particles danced in graceful spirals, their gentle movements adding a touch of magic to the stillness of the morning. The dust, suspended in the warm golden light, retained the energy from the previous night's ceremony, marking the sacred work and profound experience that had unfolded. The air felt fresh, calm, and alive with potential as the earth rejuvenated its energy with the arrival of dawn.

The entire jungle outside exhaled a collective sigh of tranquility. The sounds of nocturnal wildlife faded into the soft melody of the morning: the gentle rustling of leaves and the distant calls of birds greeting the day. A harmony settled in the atmosphere, inviting quiet reflection on the night that had passed and gently signaling a transition into a new day filled with peace. Nature orchestrated a symphony of rest and rejuvenation, creating a harmonious balance between the sacred stillness within the maloca and the vibrant life outside in the jungle.

The warmth of the morning light encircled me like a tender embrace, dissolving any lingering tension from the night before. As the first rays washed over the maloca, a wave of gratitude and reverence flooded over me for both the space and the journey I had undertaken within it. The air, rich with the scents of the jungle, felt pure and healing, intertwining with light to herald a fresh beginning. This sacred moment unveiled the beauty and serenity following transformation—a quiet peace emerging from the depths of the profound experiences of the night.

With quiet grace, the lady shaman stood at the heart of the meadow, her demeanor poised and tranquil, patiently awaiting each of us for the ceremonial flower bath. Her presence emanated calmness, a nurturing aura of wisdom that transcended the ages. Her movements flowed deliberately, harmonizing with the rhythm of the earth, steeped in ancient knowledge that defied words. Her gaze, soft yet penetrating, held countless worlds of understanding, witnessing innumerable souls through the passage of time. Her presence cultivated an environment of safety, encompassing the profound mysteries of life and death.

I stepped forward slowly, with respect, recognizing this moment as more than ritual; it became a sacred act of purification, a deeper plunge into the unknown. The shaman approached with a bowl nestled in her hands, the water within glimmering like moonlit reflections. Infused with fragrant petals and revered herbs, the water had drawn energy under the gentle moonlight, absorbing its transformative essence. The freshly gathered herbs contained the very life force of the jungle—earthy, vibrant, and potent.

As the water poured over my head, its coolness harmonized with the morning warmth, playing a refreshing and comforting melody. Each drop bore the spirit of the earth, the essence of the jungle, and the profound wisdom of the plants. Water mixed with petals cascaded down my face and body, leaving trails of tranquility and serenity. The blossoms' sweet, evocative aroma filled the air, grounding and elevating me, connecting my breaths to the heartbeat of the earth beneath.

The atmosphere brimmed with the mingling fragrances of earth and flowers, each inhalation deepening my sense of profound peace. The scent carried the essence of the jungle, along with ancient wisdom and healing energy. Damp earth and fresh blossoms intertwined to create a sacred ambiance where the physical and spiritual realms fused seamlessly. The curandera's gentle touch enveloped me not merely in water but in the very essence of life. Each drop stripped away layers of doubt, fear, and uncertainty, leaving me lighter and more attuned to the natural world. Through her hands, the jungle welcomed me back, inviting me to embrace the harmony and balance lying beneath the surface.

Gratitude surged through me, its depth nearly overwhelming. Tears welled in my eyes as I bowed in silent reverence for the sacredness of this moment. Every fiber of my being touched a divine purity that echoed within my soul. My heart expanded, connecting with something greater than myself—timeless, eternal, and ineffable.

The ritual possessed power beyond description within its uncomplicated essence. Accepting the flower bath transcended mere physical cleansing, evolving into an intimate communion with the spirit of the jungle, the plants, and their age-old wisdom. Every drop of water and falling petal carried the earth's essence, anchoring and elevating me in a single breath. The water flowed over my skin, washing away the weight I had borne—fears, doubts, and confusions dissolving layer by layer, rendering me lighter and freer.

This sacred moment dismantled everything I believed I knew about myself, stripping away false identities and accumulated grief. What remained was luminous and whole—an essence concealed beneath a stormy surface of chaos. The purification went beyond mere physicality; it awakened a spiritual vitality that revived the truest aspect of my being. I recognized that we exist beyond our past, beyond the traumas we carry or the stories we narrate, thriving within the infinite presence held within us all.

As the ritual concluded, I stood bathed in both physical and spiritual light, unified with everything around me. The air, rich with the scents of blossoms and earth, pulsated with living energy, connecting me to the land, its people, and the greater mysteries of life. I had morphed into an integral part of the sacred weave of existence, no longer an isolated individual wrestling for understanding. My heart, once weighed down by uncertainty, now overflowed with waves of gratitude and love. The ceremony profoundly humbled me, guiding me through healing and connection to something vast and unfathomable. For the first time, I beheld the world through clear eyes and an open heart, deeply aware that everything flowed in its rightful place.

Curiosity and wonder compelled me to check my Ōura ring, seeking insights from the extraordinary night's journey. The display revealed something incomprehensible—during my encounter with "death," my vital signs had flatlined entirely. The readings exhibited no signs of life, signaling my crossing from the living realm into the ethereal. The device recorded nothing during those moments—no heartbeat, breath, or movement—only an eerie silence, my being absent from the physical domain.

I remained transfixed by the screen as comprehension unfolded. This experience surpassed mere vivid dreams or trance states; I had authentically departed the physical realm. In those fleeting instances, my spirit ventured beyond flesh into an infinite abyss. The sensation of crossing into sacredness lingered as I processed the data. This truth transcended metaphor, manifesting as a tangible reality, offering insights that eluded ordinary understanding.

I was alive, breathing, fully aware, and my body and mind were intact. The contrast between those lifeless readings and being alive revealed a pure miracle. I returned from the brink of oblivion, transformed beyond expression. My fleeting encounter with vastness and timelessness fundamentally altered me. This experience left me humbled before the mysteries of life—endless depths remained to explore and comprehend. One truth burned brightly: my life had changed irrevocably, and the insights I had glimpsed were now engraved within my soul, guiding me toward a deeper understanding of both self and universe.

The ceremony concluded, yet the quiet aftermath reverberated with an unfolding journey. Though the maloca fell silent, the echoes of the night resonated within me. The lessons imparted, the transformations ignited, and the spiritual awakening I witnessed marked only the initial steps in an unimaginably expansive process. A vast doorway had opened, leaving me at its threshold, poised to embrace whatever would emerge next.

As the day unfolded, an air of curious unease surged through me. The jungle surrounding our sanctuary throbbed with a tangible and unusual energy. The ceremony's power had awakened the spirit of the land. Strolling along the paths, I encountered snakes—many in diverse shapes, sizes, and colors—gliding across the ground and curling around branches with deliberate elegance. Their scales gleamed in the dappled sunlight streaming through the thick canopy. The sight held me captive; the jungle thrummed with life, each creature moving in sync with an unseen rhythm. Snakes appeared everywhere, their presence sacred, as if they were carriers of the jungle's spirit, bearing important messages.

The facilitators, seasoned guardians of this vibrant landscape who had participated in countless ceremonies, observed in astonishment. They had never witnessed such an assembly of snakes. Their presence bore immense significance—this gathering transcended ordinary encounters. These sightings articulated the jungle's energy, elevated by our ceremony. The earth had absorbed our sacred night, and nature responded in kind.

The jungle became increasingly lively, more animated than I had ever seen. Beyond the familiar sounds of insects and distant bird calls, an intangible essence enhanced everything—revealing a world intricately linked to greater forces. The snakes embodied this energy, moving purposefully through the landscape as living emblems of transformation. The air thickened with meaning; every step served as a reminder that my journey extended beyond the personal narrative, diving into the expansive realms of existence—a calling from both the jungle and the medicine to delve into the mysteries of life.

These serpentine visitors transcended ordinary beings, possessing deep spiritual significance. Their arrival echoed the transformational energy from my ceremony—representing cycles of life and death, shedding old skins, and rebirth. Ancient customs revere snakes as symbols of change, wisdom, and renewal. They moved through the jungle with sacred intent, their fluid, deliberate motions performing a ritual dance bridging the earth and the Divine.

Walking deliberately through the sanctuary filled me with reverence. The serpents did not arrive to instill fear but to remind me of the sacred energies unleashed during the previous night's ceremony. Their presence reflected confirmations of mystical workings rather than ominous warnings. They coiled and twisted through the underbrush, gliding seamlessly as if weaving threads between the earthly and the transcendent. Their energy bore weight; each movement marked the transformation unfolding within me and the very fabric of reality.

This moment transcended the ordinary; it manifested my spiritual journey in the physical domain. The serpents symbolized the ceremonial forces of death, rebirth, and transformation. Their unusual gathering near the sanctuary affirmed that the healing and awakening had only just begun. They guided me through the realms seen and unseen, encouraging trust in the cycles of existence and the eternal flow between life and death, as well as beginning and ending.

As I walked through the sanctuary, a deeper understanding dawned upon me—the serpents danced as part of a grand mystical choreography. They transcended simple creatures of the earth, serving as divine messengers linking humanity and the spirit world. They embodied my inner labor, shedding old layers, uncovering hidden wisdom, and inviting trust in the continuous transformation. This moment illustrated the divine connection from the previous night, interwoven into the very fabric of existence, bridging the sacred and the profane.

Chapter Two

The Serpent God

After a day filled with rest and contemplation, I returned to the maloca for my second Ayahuasca ceremony. The night breeze buzzed with electrifying vitality as if the jungle held its breath, eager for the unfolding experience. The gentle candlelight bathed the maloca in a soft glow, casting shadows that danced among our souls. The shaman, a woman with a voice like a celestial choir, invoked the stars with her songs. Her icaros echoed through the darkness, forming a sacred lullaby that enveloped the space with both serenity and strength.

I drank the thick, bitter Ayahuasca brew, its earthy essence lingering on my palate as I succumbed to familiar anticipation. My stomach was knotted with a mixture of excitement and trepidation. Within thirty minutes, the contours of my reality began to blur and fade. The flickering flame, the jungle's whispers, and the shaman's soothing chants melded into a serene oblivion. I felt myself being drawn into an alternate dimension.

In an instant, I was immersed in a breathtaking, ethereal realm—alive with light and vibrant energy. The air gleamed with a spectrum of colors more brilliant than anything I had previously encountered, each hue blending seamlessly into the next. Multidimensional shapes, ever-shifting and swirling, encircled me, their elaborate forms engaging in a timeless dance. These structures exuded life, their pulsating being resonating within me as if I had stepped into the very essence of creation.

Time lost its significance, vanishing completely. My physical form dissolved, releasing me from the constraints of earthly existence. Free and unshackled, I stood as a visitor in this dynamic realm, an observer of its wondrous unfolding. The vast, intricate tapestry stretched out before me, filled with surreal beauty. This world surged toward me, drawing me into its unending flow of grace and wonder. It felt alien, populated with extraordinary shapes and forms that seemed alive, each eager to unveil the wonders of this parallel plane of existence.

"Please, show me more," I murmured, my voice quivering in awe of the magnificence around me. The beauty overwhelmed me—a constantly evolving orchestra of colors and forms pulsing in sync with the heart of the cosmos. I stood at the precipice of endless mysteries, driven by a burning desire to see, know, and understand.

The journey deepened, pulling me into realms of limitless wonder. Shapes and patterns whirled around me, each intricate and luminous, steering me through the fundamental secrets of existence. My soul ignited with wonder and humility, yearning for more revelations from this divine source. I craved the whole experience, eager to unveil the layers of reality that lay beyond the veil of mundane perception.

This insatiable thirst for clarity compelled me to drink a second cup of Ayahuasca. In surrendering myself entirely, I relinquished control of the experience. The energy around me transformed, thickening and vibrating with an almost palpable intensity. The atmosphere thrummed with an ancient presence. To my right, I sensed a male energy unlike any I had previously encountered, radiating profound wisdom, strength, and a timeless understanding—a being that had endured through countless lifetimes, bearing the weight of history and knowledge beyond human grasp.

This presence was unprecedented—striking yet gentle, exuding an energy that demanded reverence not through assertiveness but through its sheer magnitude, a subtle authority echoing through the very fabric of reality. It felt like a profound invitation, summoning me to confront something sacred and true—an aspect I had simultaneously desired and feared.

As I stood in this moment of wonder and uncertainty, I recognized that this presence was not to be overlooked or resisted. My very essence acknowledged it: an ancient soul destined to enlighten, unveil truths, and offer guidance. The stillness around me amplified its significance, as if the entire universe paused in expectation, waiting for the next revelation.

I prepared myself for what lay ahead. Every instinct urged me to recognize this pivotal moment, one that would greatly influence my ongoing journey. A quiet certainty permeated the atmosphere, a knowing that whatever insights awaited me would resonate deeply, leaving indelible marks upon my soul. This experience transcended the ordinary; it was the convergence of the Divine and humanity, a space where the boundaries between the known and the unknown blurred, allowing the universe's mysteries to unravel in ways I could not yet grasp.

In that serene stillness, I opened myself to the flow of energy surrounding me. I felt the weight of every experience echoing before this moment—the endless searches, the lingering questions, the longing for deeper meaning. Standing there before this presence, I realized that the answers I sought were no longer distant but existed within this very moment. I was ready.

A deep, resounding voice resonated within my mind, "What do you want to know?" The power of the question sent shivers through my spine. I paused, the gravity of the moment weighing heavily upon me, before finally answering, "What is consciousness?"

In an instant, I was propelled into an infinite expanse of space, unbound and liberated from form. My physical existence dissolved, leaving me as a formless essence. I floated effortlessly through a realm where time, space, and identity evaporated, rendering them utterly insignificant. This complete liberation made every earthly attachment seem inconsequential.

What lay before me was not merely a vision but a vast field of being, a spectrum of existence that expanded endlessly. It was an ocean of vital energy, infinitely expansive and alive, with an awareness so profound that my sense of self began to dissolve.

This was not an empty void, as I had previously envisioned space; rather, it was a pulsating expanse of pure knowledge. Every fragment of this reality was interconnected in perfect harmony, moving and flowing with an ancient rhythm.

The energy within this realm overflowed with pure knowledge, awareness, and sentience. It welcomed me into the heart of existence, where the illusion separating the individual from the whole faded away. Confusion and ignorance had no place here; everything expressed an unadulterated truth. This clarity struck me with overwhelming understanding —not merely intellectual but a visceral realization that permeated my soul, intertwining my being with the infinite expanse surrounding me.

In this realm, desire felt absent, as if every longing and craving had faded into nothingness, leaving behind an expansive quietude. There was no restless quest for meaning or fulfillment. Instead, the knowledge that everything was inherently understood enveloped me, and in its place remained profound serenity—pure, unbounded bliss that arose from simply existing. It was pure awareness that radiated infinitely outward, embodying the very nature of existence and infusing every inch of the universe with its gentle presence.

Within this state of awareness, I perceived that all I had once deemed essential—pursuing ambitions, amassing wisdom, seeking validation—was merely a distraction diverting me from the deep tranquility present in both myself and the cosmos. The need for answers dissipated, for they were inherently woven into the fabric of this luminous reality. All the inquiries that had consumed me gradually fell away, revealing a truth long within my grasp, waiting patiently for me to cease my relentless chase and embrace simply being. In this vast ocean of consciousness, I felt seamlessly whole, intimately connected, and profoundly at home.

Though surrounded by an immense expanse of solitude, loneliness was absent. Instead, I was enveloped in a significant sense of unity, a profound bond that transcended any illusion of separation. The infinite space around me was infused with a comforting warmth that embraced my being. No other souls were present, nor were there conversations to engage in; yet, within this boundless void, the absence of external beings crafted a rich fullness.

This stillness was vibrant and alive, with a pervasive presence that infused the surroundings. This paradox of emptiness was not a vacancy; instead, it was a living expanse, cradling all within. Every distant galaxy, star, and fundamental particle manifested within this immense field of awareness existed in an eternal embrace, interwoven in a magnificent, limitless design that spanned existence.

As I delved into this profound understanding, the boundaries separating my self from the boundless expanse of existence began to fade. My identity softly merged with the vastness, becoming pure consciousness. The concept of "I" lost its significance as the observer intertwined with the observed became a singular entity. The illusion of separation collapsed, unveiling a startling reality: I did not merely exist as a distinct being; I was consciousness itself, experiencing the intricacies of life in a moment of profound awareness.

I had become the infinity of awareness, an uninterrupted continuum of existence. Time and space ceased their usual confines. There was no past or future—only an eternal present stretching infinitely beyond human comprehension. My body and thoughts no longer confined me. I floated in an expansive awareness where identity and limitation evaporated. I had merged into boundless consciousness, existing beyond time, form, and everything that could be categorized.

I embodied the infinite awareness that embraced the universe itself. The vast cosmos, with its complexities and intricacies, was both contained within and permeated by limitless consciousness, and I was that. Everything—the stars, galaxies, and the essence of being—lay within me, unfolding as a manifestation of my boundless awareness. I was not a detached observer; I was the awareness that allowed the universe to exist. The universe, which appeared real but did not hold the same reality as consciousness, unfolded within me, alive and breathing in the expansive landscape of my consciousness. I felt the profound depths of existence as an inseparable aspect of this unending presence, aware that everything existed within me while I transcended them all.

The realization overwhelmed me, yet it ushered in a deep peace I had never known. I had unearthed a truth hidden in my spirit, one that had perennially existed beneath layers of illusion and distraction. I felt embraced by an eternal presence, safe and nurtured as a child cradled within the womb—entirely protected by an energy far beyond human understanding. There was no fear, no uncertainty—

only the quiet embrace of a love that transcended time itself.

As I drifted further into this vast ocean of awareness, the idea of separation dissolved completely. No longer was there an "I" observing from afar; I embodied the very essence of consciousness itself, holding the entire universe within my being. The once-clear boundaries defining myself and everything beyond me vanished, revealing an infinite unity. I had become the vessel containing all existence, devoid of the distinction between the observer and the observed. This was not an abstract notion but a living reality flowing through my being.

I was pure consciousness—boundless existence and bliss. No longer tethered by physical form, I existed as unadulterated awareness, transcending all known limits. Freedom wasn't something I chased; it simply was. Longings, wishes, and desires disappeared, replaced by the serene understanding that everything I sought existed within the fullness of being. I no longer searched; I simply experienced existence wholly and effortlessly. At that moment, an unspoken joy enveloped me, so profound that it rendered all else irrelevant. Simply being was enough; it was everything.

Turning my gaze leftward, I saw a captivating sight: four majestic serpents gracefully playing in the ethereal space. Each serpent glided with its particular rhythm, crafting a mesmerizing tapestry of color and motion. A brilliant emerald snake sparkled like dew-kissed leaves; next to it, a deep crimson serpent burned with fiery vitality. A cobalt blue snake twisted elegantly among them, its scales reflecting light in enchanting patterns. An additional serpent, shimmering with golden radiance, coiled and danced through the celestial expanse, completing this stunning tableau. Together, these four breathtaking beings formed a living mosaic of color, their movements synchronized in a cosmic play that transcended earthly comprehension. Each serpent symbolized a unique facet of nature's exquisite beauty—the verdant life force of the green, the dynamic energy of the red, the profound wisdom of the blue, and the divine luminosity of the gold.

In the center stood a commanding presence: a majestic hooded cobra, its black and gray scales gleaming with otherworldly brilliance. It radiated an aura of divine authority; its energy shifted the space around it. The cobra's gaze carried a gravitas that commanded respect and reverence. Standing motionless with its hood fully extended, its eyes pierced the cosmos, fixated on a distant point in the universe. The other snakes danced playfully, weaving through the void, while the cobra remained steadfast and intensely focused.

As I remained transfixed, an extraordinary spectacle arose. Before the cobra, a galaxy ignited into motion, its stars spiraling in an elegant cadence. The cobra held vigilant watch over this celestial unfolding, its stance alert and purposeful. The galaxy glowed and throbbed with vibrant energy, casting radiant light into the cosmic canvas, while the serpent's steady focus underscored its role as a guardian of this divine realm. Each rotation of stars and every burst of light were met with the cobra's watchful gaze as it fulfilled an ancient responsibility to safeguard and observe. This magnificent being did not merely bear witness to the galaxy's birth; it served as a timeless protector of this celestial play, comprehending the mysteries of existence in ways bereft of human understanding. Through its constant vigilance, I perceived that the cobra embodied a guardian spirit, nurturing the delicate balance of cosmic forces in harmonious equilibrium.

There existed a profound bond between the cobra and the cosmos; one was rooted in the earth while the other soared in the heavens. The cobra's resolute gaze embodied ancient wisdom. It transcended mere physicality, symbolizing a divine, eternal essence. The interaction between the cobra and the cosmos resembled a celestial ballet, a harmonious relationship that unified the terrestrial and the ethereal, the familiar and the mysterious.

This moment was not by chance. The serpents and the galaxy—they were all part of the intricate weave of reality, imparting insights into timeless knowledge, harmony, and interconnectedness among all entities. The cobra, in its stillness, embodied the eternal observer, watching over the vastness of creation with both reverence and understanding. As I gazed at the cosmic display, I witnessed the very fabric of existence being laid bare. The cobra was not merely a creature of myth or symbolism; it was a guardian of cosmic truths, holding the key to an ancient, unspoken knowledge that was now being shared with me.

I advanced cautiously, each step intentional as I approached the stunning scene unfolding before me. The serpents, vivid and iridescent beings, spread throughout the sacred space, each more enchanting than the last. Their scales glimmered in a spectrum of tones, sparkling in the ambient light like precious gemstones. As I drew nearer, their movements slowed; they acknowledged my presence and chose to observe rather than continue their playful dance. Their slender bodies gracefully navigated the air, exuding a mesmerizing elegance.

It was their eyes that captivated my attention the most. Each snake's gaze was sharp and focused, fixated on me with a sentient intensity. I could feel their eyes tracing my every movement as though they were reading my intentions, my energy, and my very soul. It was an unspoken connection, a silent acknowledgment that resonated through the space around me. The awareness in their gaze sent a ripple of energy through the space—a charge that reverberated deep within my being. They granted me permission to enter their sacred habitat, where time and perception blurred and the boundaries between the physical and spiritual worlds dissolved.

The atmosphere thrummed with vibrant energy, potent yet pleasantly balanced. The presence around me radiated not discomfort but rather an ancient, sacred essence. Their domain exuded profound sanctity. A sense of reverence was palpable as if the universe itself paused in respect for the beings that graced this space.

This was a holy domain where the profane and the Divine met. The snakes were not merely physical beings; they represented something far grander. They were age-old spirits linked to nature's forces and invisible realms, and in their presence, I stood at the brink of the Sacred.

The significance of the moment and the silent connection between us humbled me. There was no urgency, no impulse to act. I simply stood, allowing the energy of the space to permeate me. This connection attuned my entire being to the surrounding energy. I became an active participant in a profound play, bearing witness to the unfolding of the divine presence. The stillness, energy, and reverence coalesced into a moment of profound clarity, revealing that this was not a mere chance encounter but a crucial experience that transcended language and understanding.

The serpents, sensing my quest for knowledge, understood my purpose. Their movements exhibited graceful intelligence as they purposefully navigated the space around me. With fluid motions, they guided me into an underground cavern, their presence both commanding and reassuring. The transition into this hidden world felt seamless yet dreamlike. The ground responded to their silent communication, shifting and revealing pathways beyond my comprehension. The cavern welcomed me as if it was extending a sacred invitation to uncover the mysteries within.

The air became denser as I ventured deeper, saturated with the essence of antiquity. I sensed a rich blend of damp stone and musk, evoking the primal essence of the underground. This atmosphere carried the weight of untold secrets, shrouding me in its timeless energy. As I journeyed onward, the heaviness intensified as though the space held mysteries yearning to be unveiled.

A soft light emanated from mineral veins embedded in the cavern's walls, casting a gentle, otherworldly glow throughout. This illumination bathed the cavern in shades of soft gold and deep green, resonating in harmony with the rhythm of the earth as if the rock breathed alongside the pulse of creation. This was a realm of extraordinary mystery, a gateway where the dimensions of time and reality blurred.

At the heart of this sacred shrine rested the black cobra, its sleek scales absorbing light that dared to penetrate the cavern's shadows. The surrounding darkness curled around the serpent, intensifying its formidable presence. Its vibrant turquoise eyes, lit with an inner flame, cut through the gloom, radiating age-old wisdom and transcending the constraints of time. The cobra was the same sentinel I had previously encountered, its awareness intricately woven into the core of existence.

Its eyes felt like portals—gateways to a realm of knowledge so profound that they defied comprehension. As I gazed into them, I confronted the universe's deepest mysteries, its concealed truths laid bare. The cobra's gaze didn't merely observe; it delved into my very core, unveiling aspects of myself that had remained hidden. Those eyes seemed to unravel my essence, peeling away layers of history, fears, and unvoiced thoughts as they measured the fullness of my existence with an intensity I could not evade.

Unexpectedly, the distance between us began to vanish. Time warped, and I no longer felt separate from the cobra. The connection we shared felt ancient, forged in realms that transcended comprehension. I stood there, humbled and awed, aware that this meeting was a sacred dialogue between the Keeper of universal truths and a wandering soul seeking its place within the vast tapestry of consciousness.

The other serpents, each more radiant and captivating than the last, adorned the main cavern wall in a formation that appeared both deliberate and organic. Their bodies glided in intricate spirals and flowing arcs, crafting a breathtaking labyrinth. The patterns they formed seemed intentional, part of a remarkable design converging toward the black cobra at the center. This living sculpture—a mosaic of serpentine forms—seemed imbued with pulsating life, moving in perfect harmony with unseen energy, a timeless masterpiece etched into the shrine's fabric. Their movement was rhythmic and enthralling—a continuous play that transcended generations yet remained forever constant.

The environment surrounding the black cobra throbbed with an unmistakable aura of divinity—a wave of spiritual energy that vibrated through the shrine. This being was not merely an inhabitant of the cavern; it represented an energy that manipulated time and space itself. Its presence emanated divine authority, saturating the chamber with a spiritual intensity that was almost tangible. The cavern resonated with the rhythm of the snakes, pulsing with the echo of ancient energies that permeated every stone and serpentine form. The walls, ceiling, and ground radiated sacredness. This was a sanctuary that transcended the familiar world—a place where the barriers between the physical and the spiritual began to dissolve.

As I stood before this majestic entity, a profound wave of reverence and awe washed over me; the very essence of divinity embraced me, a humbling and overwhelming energy. My entire being felt anchored by the significance of the moment, yet simultaneously, an overwhelming tranquility filled the air, a quiet acceptance that this was where I was destined to be. The energy throughout the temple pulsed with such intensity and depth that it dispelled all uncertainty. It was undeniable: I stood in the presence of something ancient and magnificent, something eternal that transcended human comprehension.

In the suspended stillness, my voice emerged as a mere whisper, and I found myself asking, "Are you God?" The question slipped from my lips, not borne of fear but rather from an earnest reverence for the divine being before me.

In an instant, I was transported to the infinite expanse of the cosmos. Here, the atmosphere wrapped around me with a sense of intimacy, as if I were in a sacred audience with a presence of immense power. Hovering above me in the void, an entity loomed large. Although I felt connected to my earthly self, I was devoid of a physical form, existing solely as energy.

The being before me had the lower body of a serpent, its scales seamlessly transitioning into a strong, elegant form. Its upper body was that of a man adorned with long, dark hair cascading over a ceremonial robe of crimson and white. Perched atop its head was a golden crown with a trident-like motif, from which radiant beams of light burst forth, illuminating the vast emptiness around us.

A deep kindness radiated from him as if he were welcoming me like an old friend, his presence infused with an aura of profound wisdom. A familiarity lingered in his gaze, a gentle yet all-knowing expression that made me feel as if I had returned home to something timeless and eternal. In disbelief at what I was witnessing, I managed to repeat my question: "Are you God?" He softly replied, "You may call me that if you wish." A surge of curiosity filled me, prompting my next question: "If you are God, whom does humanity worship?" His eyes sparkled with a touch of humor as he playfully responded, "Whom do you think?"

I said, "This is the greatest joke on humanity," in reaction to the profound realization that the serpent, once a revered symbol in ancient traditions, had been misunderstood and misrepresented over time. In religious texts, it had been demonized and portrayed as a tempter or a symbol of evil. In reality, however, the serpent embodied transformation, knowledge, and awakening—qualities that humanity desperately needed to reclaim. Those who distorted its role in these texts, twisting its symbolism into something to fear and divide, had done humanity a great disservice. To this, he responded, "You've understood it."

The realization crashed upon me like a thunderclap, leading to an uncontrollable fit of laughter. I struggled to contain it, mindful of the disruption I might be causing to the others in the maloca. Yet, I could not repress the joy erupting from within—a celebration of finally grasping the essence of a cosmic truth.

I found myself face to face with the Serpent God, his face mere inches from mine, and our eyes locked in a profound connection that whispered ancient knowledge. I remained still, soaking in this deep bond, and queried, "What fate awaits humanity?" The timeless being's eyes darkened with an indescribable sorrow, and his commanding presence dimmed as waves of grief coursed through his ethereal form. "There is nothing I can do," the deity lamented, his voice heavy with the weight of ages past.

The depth of his sorrow transcended mere expression; it embodied a cosmic grief that echoed across the essence of reality. In his gaze, I perceived the burden of understanding humanity's trajectory while being shackled by the unyielding laws that barred him from intervention. I pressed on, "Will civilization destroy itself again, as it has in the past?" Silence reigned. No reply. One more attempt escaped my lips: "Is this a consequence of religion?" Still, there was no response; only a profound aura of inevitability lingered in the air.

The monumental nature of this cosmic encounter filled me with acute clarity. I had to safeguard this knowledge. "I'm afraid I may forget these insights. Can I share them with someone and come back?" I asked. My inquiry conveyed a heartfelt desire to honor this sacred knowledge by imparting it before my human recollection could fade. He nodded. I withdrew from the vision, approached a facilitator, and breathlessly urged, "If I forget by tomorrow, please remind me that I said God resembles a serpent."

When I returned to the Serpent God, who awaited patiently, an indescribable calm enveloped me. In his presence, all the questions that once buzzed around my mind dissipated into silence. His tranquil yet commanding energy echoed within me, ushering in a state of quiet understanding. However, my scientific curiosity sparked anew. Unable to hold back, I gazed upon him, my eyes aglow with wonder, and asked, "Will you allow me to explore other realities?" He regarded me with a gentle, amused smile and answered, "What would you like to see? Fireworks?"

For a fleeting moment, I felt the weight of my foolishness in desiring to visit other parallel universes while in the company of the Divine. "Forgive me," I pleaded. "I wish only to remain in your presence." The Serpent God acquiesced, rising to rest upon a massive golden slab that floated in the vast expanse of the cosmic void.

He stood with his body coiled, taking the form of a hooded cobra; his posture mirrored the grace and power of the serpent. He stood tall and resolute, his body poised as if suspended between the worlds, channeling energy so vast that it rippled outward in waves of pure, divine light. His eyes were closed, yet his presence seemed to pierce through the very fabric of reality, an undeniable energy that filled the emptiness around him.

The scene changed, revealing my transformation into a monk clad in vibrant orange robes, my head cleanly shaved. I sat cross-legged at the base of the floating golden platform, submerged in meditation, while a perfect sphere of golden light enveloped me. Within that sacred sphere, waves of comfort and tranquility flooded my being as if I had discovered my true sanctuary in the boundless infinity.

Suddenly, I became aware of a feminine presence surrounding me. Though unseen, her essence resonated as radiant, nurturing energy overflowing with a maternal love that transcended all earthly experiences. It was an embrace so profound and sustaining that it encompassed the core of every comforting moment I had ever known, distilled into this single divine instance. A gentle touch graced my shoulder, sending currents of unconditional love surging through me.

Her voice, soft and tender, wrapped around me like a lullaby. "Let's leave God alone," she whispered. "Come with me." Then, with an unearthly compassion that cradled my soul, she asked softly, "Do you want to know why you suffer?" "Yes," I replied, my voice trembling.

Instantly, she transported me thirty years back to a fateful car accident. I sat in the back seat alongside my pregnant fiancée when the driver lost control. While she survived the initial impact, she succumbed to her injuries a week later. Mother Ayahuasca revealed to me her lifeless form, placed side by side with a newborn she called "baby Alexander," on the green grass just a few feet away from the wreckage. She consoled me, saying, "You've always blamed yourself, but it wasn't your fault. You tried to save them. Events must follow a certain path."

For the first time, I allowed my grief to surface fully. My heart ached, yet within that release lay healing. Mother Ayahuasca held space for me until my sorrow subsided, softly whispering, "You have to let it go." With that endless maternal love in her gaze, she inquired, "Do you want to know more?" Without hesitation, I responded, "Yes."

In an instant, I was transported to my previous life, vividly reliving the moments of my service in the military. The scene unfolded with startling clarity. I stood side by side with a familiar figure—a spiritual brother who was participating in the ceremony—dressed in military fatigues and wearing Naval Special Forces patches. He was my best friend, and I was his commanding officer. We were at the military base, preparing for a covert operation; the atmosphere was filled with tension. The familiar sounds of the base surrounded us: the heavy clanking of equipment, the rustling of gear, and the quiet buzz of urgency before a deployment. We walked, exchanging no words, but our focus was absolute. We were ready.

Soon, we plunged into the cold, dark ocean, and the shock of entry reverberated throughout my body. Before me, three other divers swam in flawless unison—members of my team making their way toward our waiting submarine. Its immense silhouette lay in the deep, barely distinguishable against the muted light filtering through the water. The eerie stillness of the underwater realm surrounded us, interrupted only by the muffled sounds of our movements and the rhythmic release of bubbles from our gear. Although this was a routine rendezvous, an unsettling intuition stirred in my gut. Something felt amiss.

My chest tightened in the very environment where I had spent countless hours training, where each action and procedure had become instinctual through relentless drills. Yet now, my breath became shallow and labored, transforming this familiar surrounding into a constrictive grip. My teammates carried on with their routines, oblivious to my unease. As every heartbeat thundered in my ears, darkness encroached upon my vision. The crushing pressure in my lungs intensified with each passing second, and my body screamed for air. Years of training faded into primal dread as my limbs felt heavy and distant. My crew moved confidently, their focus on the mission preventing them from noticing my silent struggle. I was overwhelmed by a suffocating reality: the waters that had once felt like home had turned inhospitable.

The frigid, weighty embrace of the ocean grew more oppressive as I gasped for breath that eluded me. Panic seized my body, and I could feel the world closing in, turning every movement sluggish and each breath more laborious than the last. The outlines of my fellow divers blurred as I fought against the engulfing darkness. I lost track of their muffled sounds and clear forms. I felt only the relentless void of the ocean, the constraining depths, and the terrifying realization that I was facing death.

As these vivid memories emerged—too precise to dismiss yet astonishing to accept—I repeatedly asked Mother Ayahuasca if this was truly real—a hidden thread that seemed to unravel so much of my being. With infinite understanding, Mother Ayahuasca guided me through a journey of discovery, illuminating the evidence laid before me. She revealed how an indescribable drive to join the Navy had taken root within me long before I could comprehend its origin. She gestured toward the military mattress I had brought on this trip, a subconscious anchor to a past life I had forgotten but never completely escaped. Each insight fell into place with striking clarity, unraveling questions I hadn't thought to ask regarding my deepest motivations and unexplainable urges.

With profound compassion, Mother Ayahuasca gazed into my soul and declared, "You died during that mission. It was an accident. You returned to validate your worth, to prove you did not fail. You have nothing to prove; you are enough." Her declaration unraveled the tightly coiled guilt I had borne for so long.

She highlighted my tattoos, the skulls that had always inexplicably captivated me. She explained that they are symbols of transformation and strength. More importantly, she said, the skulls also embody the principle of choosing death before dishonor—a commitment to honor and integrity above all else. "These are echoes of your past," she explained. "They are remnants of a life you no longer need to hold onto. Release them; they no longer serve you."

With that, I began to purge, expelling lifetimes of guilt and the weight of an unfulfilled mission. Each convulsion released not just physical discomfort but also the deep-seated shadows and karmic ties that had been embedded in my very soul. When the purging ended, an incredible sense of relief and liberation engulfed me, as if I had discarded chains I had been unknowingly shackled to.

Emerging from the maloca and stepping into the jungle felt like a profound invitation—a deep, unmistakable urge to return to a place that had always been my true home. As I ventured into this vibrant realm, a powerful sense of belonging wrapped around me. The jungle welcomed me, its air buzzing with dynamic energy that coursed through my soul. The rustling foliage murmured its greeting while the nocturnal chorus communicated with a resonance that stirred my very spirit. The dense greenery, the rich aroma of moist earth, and the warm, sultry night enveloped me like a cherished embrace, rekindling memories of countless lifetimes that flourished in this hallowed space.

As I ventured deeper into the jungle, the sensation of connection deepened. The gentle swaying of trees, distant animal calls, and the hum of insects interwove into a vibrant tapestry, becoming a part of me as much as my heartbeat. It was a realm that embraced my essence, a sacred space where my identity merged seamlessly with the natural world.

Above me, the sky stretched infinitely, adorned with stars that sparkled brightly, almost within reach, casting a silvery sheen across the jungle. Each star glowed fiercely, making the cosmos feel intimate and alive. The constellations whispered secrets of the universe that I understood in ways that transcended logic.

Though the ceremony had concluded, the jungle cradled me as if it had awaited my return for eons. My heart began to heal, and with newfound serenity, I returned to the maloca to rest, allowing myself to be enveloped by Mother Ayahuasca's nurturing presence. As I drifted into a restorative, dreamless sleep, I felt an unbreakable bond with the world around me, cradled by the stars and serenaded by the vibrant spirit of the Amazonian jungle.

The next day, the curandera awaited me with a tranquil, knowing aura, holding a basin filled with water infused with petals and sacred herbs steeped under the moonlight. She initiated the ritual, gently pouring the fragrant water over my head, causing a cool cascade to flow down my face and body. The air blossomed with a sweet, earthy perfume mingling with the refreshing breath of the jungle. Each drop was a blessing, cleansing not only my physical form but also washing away layers of emotional detritus, pain, and weight I had unknowingly carried for ages.

As the water streamed over me, I closed my eyes to fully immerse myself in the moment, embracing the sense of renewal that consumed me. The curandera's soothing voice harmonized with the rustling leaves and the gentle serenade of morning birds, creating a symphony that resonated within my soul. It felt as if the jungle itself participated in this sacred purification, offering its vibrant essence to the healing process. The floral bath became a rebirth, a ritual honoring the release of old wounds and welcoming the emergence of a more illuminated self.

With every droplet that caressed my skin, layers of past traumas and self-doubt began to dissolve, replaced by an overwhelming sensation of peace and gratitude. Warmth blossomed in my heart, and clarity flooded my mind. I recognized that a profound shift had occurred within me—a deep-rooted feeling of returning to myself, reclaiming aspects of my soul that had been lost or buried over time.

This journey drew me closer to the essence of who I am, unveiling transformative truths within. I felt whole. No longer did I sense a void or something amiss. Instead, I experienced completeness, a beautiful tapestry woven from each experience, every lesson, and every ounce of love and wisdom shared with me. The sense of unity and harmony surged within me, and a quiet, powerful joy radiated from me, akin to the warm brilliance of the morning sun.

Chapter Three

The Warrior's Sacrifice

My third Ayahuasca ceremony started under the vigilant guidance of the same two shamans who had facilitated our initial ceremony. Their presence provided reassurance and a sense of stability, anchoring me as change loomed on the horizon. The maloca thrummed with energy vibrating from both the earth below and the expansive canopy above. The walls seemed to absorb the intensity of our shared anticipation while the jungle outside hummed with a similar electric charge.

As the shamans set the stage with fluid, practiced movements, I felt the weight of the ritual embracing me. The familiar sounds of the jungle—the chittering of insects and distant animal calls—began to fade, yielding to the profound, unseen rhythms of the ceremony. Each sound resonated with significance, merging into a haunting orchestra of whispers that beckoned us toward the undiscovered. Within this potent ambiance, I settled onto the mat, ready to embark on this new experience.

When the moment arrived, I drank the thick, bitter brew. Its sharp taste was a familiar yet unwelcome reminder that my body was fully awake and aware. As I swallowed, the liquid spread through me, signaling that a sacred experience was at hand. The brew coursed through me, settling deep within my core and radiating warmth and discomfort throughout. I sensed the plant medicine unraveling the dormant energies inside, stirring memories of previous ceremonies. As my breath steadied, a palpable stillness enveloped the space.

As I sank deeper into the experience, I awaited the arrival of Mother Ayahuasca, feeling those familiar waves of anxiety and expectation flooding me. I closed my eyes, attempting to surrender to the unfolding journey, yet a reluctant part of me hesitated, unsure and tentative. The knot in my stomach tightened, but I recognized it as a necessary part of the process—a crucial milestone on the path to deeper insights. The sensation of something vast and transcendent lingered just beyond my awareness, ready to envelop me. The jungle outside pulsed in rhythm with my breath, a reminder that I was not embarking on this journey alone.

Time lost its rigidity and melted into fluidity as I awaited the medicine's revelations. Each breath felt heavy, a reminder of the moment's weight pressing down upon me. I urged myself to remain open, trusting in the unfolding process and surrendering to Mother Ayahuasca's guidance. The air inside the maloca buzzed with energy, the earthy aroma mingling with the sharp scent of the brew and the incense the shamans burned. The walls enveloped us not with confinement but with the sacred intensity of our collective experience, drawing me closer to a momentous transformation.

After what seemed like an eternity, vivid clarity surged through me; the barrier between this world and the next had finally dissolved, granting me insight. The other participants, once mere fellow travelers on this path, metamorphosed into something of profound importance—my teammates, my brothers-in-arms from the previous experience. The connection we shared was deep and transcendent; we were no longer strangers but were bonded as one. While we had arrived as individuals, in that moment, I recognized the undeniable truth that we belonged to something far grander.

Scanning the room, I sensed the weight of their suffering, palpable and nearly suffocating. Each individual wrestled with personal struggles, purging into their buckets with intense force, their bodies quaking with the exertion of release. I could hear their muffled sobs, raw and heart-wrenching, breaking through the heavy atmosphere of the maloca. They were not merely facing physical discomfort; they confronted profound, ancient pain long buried within. Their grief loomed like a dark cloud overhead, oppressive, and my heart ached for them in ways that were difficult to articulate.

My sense of self further dissolved, replaced by a profound surge of compassion for those souls who struggled as I had. Their anguish became my own, as if the boundaries between us had vanished. I felt their pain coursing through me, unbearable in its resonance. My usually cluttered mind cleared in a fleeting moment, prompting me to call out inwardly to the one being I knew could offer solace: Mother Ayahuasca.

In a moment of urgency, I quietly implored, making a heartfelt supplication: "Please, Mother, heal my crew." These words emerged from a place of profound love but also gravity, imbued with the weight of my soul's understanding. I yearned to witness their healing, to see them liberated from their anguish, and to feel them discover peace.

I had interlaced myself into their struggle, and in turn, their pain transformed into my sacred mission. The ceremony had evolved into not just an individual journey of healing but a collective experience of compassion and unity. I could no longer separate myself from their paths, and in that realization, I understood that my intentions needed to bear the weight of our shared healing. I pleaded with every fiber of my being for divine assistance, asking for guidance toward the light that awaited on the other side of our suffering.

A torrent of words surged forth from me as if they had long awaited their release. A wellspring of strength inside had opened, and the words flowed with uncontainable power. I could not contain them, nor did I wish to. My voice resonated with intensity, clear and strong, imbued with a force that was both familiar and inexplicable.

"Don't you ever forget that you are the greatest warriors," I proclaimed, my voice steadfast yet charged with fervor. "You are the bravest, the strongest, the most trained." Each statement resonated with authenticity, transcending mere physicality and delving into the essence of my being. I felt the weight of these words resonate in the shared space, echoing off the maloca's walls, infusing the atmosphere with purpose and intent.

"You can achieve anything you set your mind to," I continued, the power of my assertion strengthening with each utterance. This was not merely encouragement; it was a call to awaken the infinite potential residing within each of us. "Go deep within," I urged, "find the tool you need, pull it out, and put it to good use."

My words flowed like a sacred incantation designed to awaken dormant strength within each participant. I spoke to them as their commander, yet not from a place of superiority but as a guide who saw the depths of their strength, even when they could not see it themselves. My words carried the conviction of someone who believed in their resilience, motivating them to rise and seize their power.

The collective energy surged, an invisible tide that lifted us all. The entire maloca inhaled deeply, exhaling past limitations while welcoming fresh possibilities. I felt grounded yet elevated, connected to something vastly greater. My words rippled through the room like waves in water, touching every individual and kindling a collective spirit that was both personal and universal. In my heart, I knew these words were meant for more than my expression; they were to be felt, embraced, and embodied by every soul present. The warrior spirit was vibrant and awake, ready for reclamation.

The resonance of my voice filled the space—not disruptively, but with an energy that seemed to penetrate the air itself. I was aware of each word I delivered, yet a force beyond me had seized control, channeling my voice as its instrument. The words cascaded effortlessly, like a river flowing on its destined course, revealing that I was merely the vessel for something more profound—an understanding beyond my own.

One of the facilitators quietly approached me, exuding a sense of calm with deliberate and soothing gestures. His hand rested gently on my shoulder, providing a reassuring presence that anchored me to the moment. This soft touch drew me back from the ethereal energy that had shrouded me. Leaning in slightly, he spoke with kindness, "Brother, please lower your voice. It may be disturbing the others." His gentle reminder underscored the significance of our shared space and collective experience.

Embarrassment swept through me as I inhaled deeply and nodded in acknowledgment. I endeavored to still my spirit, returning my energy to a place of tranquility and humility. As I sat there, the warmth of his hand lingered on my shoulder. I sensed a significant transformation in the atmosphere; the heightened energy from my outburst began to settle, not diminishing but recalibrating the entire environment. It felt as though I had sparked a shift, stirring something within the maloca that blossomed into a more refined, grounded essence. Humbled yet grateful, I connected with the vibrant energy pulsating around me, now more alive than ever.

Seated on my mat, I sensed reality itself shifting. What I once recognized morphed into a breathtaking kaleidoscope of colors, each hue throbbing with vitality. The walls of the maloca, the floor beneath me, and the surrounding objects appeared to dissolve and reform in a fluid, continuous dance. The shapes around me were distorted and pixelated, like shards of light converging to create new forms, only to reassemble into something entirely different. Every surface radiated vibrant energy; even the atoms composing the objects inside the maloca vibrated in harmony with the universe itself.

The unfolding colors transcended expression, surpassing anything I had previously envisioned while feeling more vivid and true than my familiar world. Deep, luxurious blues flowed effortlessly into fiery oranges, their edges glowing with enchanting light. Brilliant purples twirled with luminous yellows, creating an orchestral masterpiece of colors that hummed with energy. Electric greens flickered like living sparks, brimming with a force that felt almost conscious. Each particle glittered with radiant light, and the emerging shapes held infinite fractal complexity: patterns within patterns, perpetually repeating and expanding in a mesmerizing interplay of orderly chaos. It felt as if the very essence of the universe had revealed itself to me, showcasing its raw, untamed beauty in a spectacular display of limitless creativity and wonder.

I could only watch in awe as my surroundings transformed into a breathtaking exhibition of cosmic artistry. Time seemed to dissolve; the moment stretched and folded in on itself, each new perspective more remarkable than the last. The intricacy of the patterns eluded comprehension yet felt entirely natural, as if I were observing the fundamental structure of reality itself.

Inundated by this profound vision, I managed to utter a single word: "Wow!" It slipped from my lips in a breathy whisper, a simple acknowledgment of the beauty and mystery unfolding around me. Yet that solitary word felt insufficient for such a transcendent experience. It was a marvel so pure and expansive that no expression could encapsulate it entirely. I surrendered to the experience, immersing myself in the ever-evolving fractals of light and energy surrounding me.

Sensing my astonishment, the curandero turned towards me without a word. With a swift, deliberate motion, he reached for the agua florida and sprayed its mist toward me. The cool spray enveloped my skin, ushering in a sensation that felt utterly magical.

As the droplets landed, the space around me transformed. The air vibrated with radiant particles, shimmering with a golden glow. The room had transfigured into a celestial sanctuary, suspended in a realm of exquisite, ethereal beauty. Golden particles floated gracefully around me, twinkling like tiny stars in a cosmic ballet. The atmosphere itself throbbed with a palpable light, enveloping the maloca in a warm, golden brilliance that felt both mystical and deeply comforting.

The boundaries separating the physical and spiritual blurred, wrapping me in divine energy. The sacred flower water, imbued with ancient, cleansing properties, not only purified the space but elevated it to a higher plane. I experienced weightlessness as if cradled by the cosmos in a golden haze. A profound sense of peace and sanctity cascaded over me as if every golden particle carried the universe's love and wisdom, pouring over me and filling my heart with overwhelming gratitude.

The entire maloca buzzed with this sacred energy, each golden particle a testament to the divine presence now within our midst. The ceremony transcended its earthly context, lifting me into a higher realm where the mundane ceased to exist. In that moment, only beauty, light, and the presence of something beyond comprehension remained—a timeless, eternal experience.

As if responding to my heartfelt yearning, Mother Ayahuasca manifested before me as a vast, permeating energy. Her presence radiated both nurturing warmth and resolute authority. She embodied the very essence of the universe: infinite yet immediate, both comforting and powerful. A deep tranquility enveloped me within her energetic embrace, accompanied by an indelible sense of knowing. She existed beyond form, living as the vibration of existence itself, filling the space with an omnipresent aura.

"You're asking me to heal them," she said, her voice a melodious blend of compassion and authority. It was a statement, not a question—an acknowledgment of the truth buried in my heart. "There's only one way this can be accomplished," she continued, her words laden with ancient wisdom. "I can transfer their doings to you, and you have to purge them. Do you want to do this, or would you prefer to return to the blissful realm you just experienced?"

Her question hung in the air, evoking a stillness akin to the calm before a storm. The choice presented was clear yet far from simple. I had just traversed a dimension of profound beauty and serenity, a realm where everything felt whole and harmonious. The temptation to revisit that euphoria was irresistible, yet the responsibility before me weighed even heavier. I felt the significance of the moment, the sacred nature of the task I was being called to embrace. This challenge was not merely physical but deeply spiritual—a call to serve and bear the suffering of others in pursuit of healing.

Without hesitation and with unyielding certainty, I replied, "I'll do it," my voice emanating from a profound inner conviction. It was more than a choice; it was a surrender, an acceptance of the burden of others' pain in hopes of facilitating healing and wholeness.

The instant I uttered those words, a portal to another realm opened before me. The path ahead was simple in its intention, yet the journey beyond remained shrouded in mystery. I recognized it as an essential part of this sacred passage—an invitation to venture beyond familiar confines. Embracing the unknown, I readied my heart and uncluttered mind to face whatever awaited me on the other side.

There was no wavering, no thought of self-preservation; only a profound determination to assist my team resonated within me. My focus rested solely on absorbing their anguish and suffering to aid in their healing. Though the weight of my choice pressed upon my chest, it felt less like a burden and more like a chosen responsibility. An overwhelming sense of duty eclipsed the potential risks.

Mother Ayahuasca asked me again, "Are you sure you want to do this?" I answered without hesitation, "Yes." It was not a moment of bravado; it was simply the right path forward. It felt as if an unseen energy—the essence of existence—had predetermined this choice, transcending fear and self-interest.

"You have to drink a second cup," Mother Ayahuasca's voice resonated in my mind, soothing yet unwavering. I nodded silently, propelled by the urgency of the moment. I asked for a second cup, its weight heavy in my palms, carrying not just the brew but also the essence of healing. The liquid sloshed thickly, its bitterness more pronounced this time. With reverence, I swallowed it, feeling it cascade down my throat and settle in my belly, igniting a fire within me.

As moments slipped by, the jungle's concerto faded, allowing me to attune to my inner self. Once more, I heard Mother Ayahuasca's voice: "Are you ready?" "Yes," I replied with conviction. There was no turning back; I had already crossed a threshold, fully engaged in the task ahead. Silence surrounded me, charged with the hum of energy swirling around. Then her voice returned, rich and knowing: "I've transferred their doings to you. Purge it out."

Her words felt like an invocation, a cosmic decree rather than mere instructions. At her command, I sensed the weight of darkness and suffering infiltrating my being, spiraling within me like a tempest. I had transformed into a vessel for the pain, unresolved traumas, and silent grief surrounding me. The energy was overwhelming, too much for a single soul to bear, yet I understood my calling. The pressure mounted within me, sickness surged, and I realized that the only path forward lay in release. I had to expel it. I had to let it all go.

Suddenly, my body spasmed, a profound force stirring something long buried within. Each fiber of my being responded to an energy greater than myself. I began purging violently, each heave pulling from depths I could not name. Wave after wave of toxic energy erupted from me, rushing out like gushing black ink. The sensation eluded description; each wave felt like the shedding of burdens, fragments of sorrow, trauma, and darkness extending back through generations. I became an agent of unraveling ancestral pain, liberating a weight that had been carried for far too long.

The purge was relentless, one wave crashing into another with no respite. Just when I thought the tide might recede, another surge of suffering erupted from my core, compelling me to release yet more. It was an overwhelming ordeal, a fierce struggle for breath and sanity, as inhalation intertwined with expelling the malign energy within. My body quaked with each purge, and every instant felt eternal, a persistent battle to cast out the darkness while anchoring myself in awareness. It felt infinite, like a vast ocean of unresolved pain and fear, drawing me into its depths with every exhalation. Yet even amidst this turmoil, an unexpected relief surfaced. The battle continued, but with each wave, I sensed myself inching closer to freeing myself of these dark energies.

As the purging subsided, the tumult of darkness, the intense upheaval, and the relentless expulsion faded into a distant echo, leaving behind an almost surreal stillness. My body once wracked with violent spasms, now lay limp and drained. Each muscle ached, trembling in the wake of the struggle. Yet paradoxically, a profound relief settled over me as if the air itself had lightened, freeing me from an oppressive weight.

The darkness I expelled manifested as both visions and visceral energy. I watched them wriggle and contort as they left my body, transforming into grotesque manifestations of fear and sorrow. They emerged from a vast inheritance of suffering passed down through unseen connections. They served as twisted mirrors of despair, striving to grasp at me, carrying not my anguish but the collective grief of those I was destined to aid. These shadows held the trauma, anger, and guilt of those I had been called to support—energies attempting to cling to their host. Instead, I became a conduit for their unresolved darkness, facilitating release.

Lying there, utterly spent, each part of me ached. My mind felt foggy, detached, yet oddly clear. Gone was the toxic energy once residing within; instead, there lingered a gentle emptiness, as if a new space had opened within me. It was not a void of loss but a renewal, a clearing for something new and pure to emerge.

In this serene aftermath, I sensed the presence of Mother Ayahuasca once again, as a nurturing energy embracing me. Her voice, tender yet resolute, resounded as if it were echoing the very essence of my soul. "You have always wanted to know who you are," she spoke, her tone gentle, revealing a truth I had long known yet had refused to acknowledge. "Now you know."

The words bore the weight of a cosmic revelation, shaking me to my core. Still reeling from the intensity of the purge, I grappled with the physical and emotional fatigue that clouded my understanding of her message. My thoughts spiraled—

Who am I?

I tried to convey that I still didn't fully understand and had not yet uncovered my true identity. However, before I could even fully form these thoughts, she had already vanished, the connection slipping away as quickly as it had come.

Her voice faded from my awareness. The jungle beyond the maloca fell silent, its sounds dwindling into a distant murmur as stillness enveloped me. While the question lingered unanswered, her words had sown a seed of understanding deep within. A fundamental awakening stirred inside, and though its whole meaning eluded me, I felt the roots of a profound truth beginning to flourish, growing stronger with every heartbeat.

The cool air of the maloca embraced me, intertwining with the residual warmth of the ceremony. Silence descended, wrapping me in a comforting shroud. Through the haze of my thoughts, I sought to gather the scattered remnants of my experience. An overarching stillness enveloped everything, creating a sacred calm as if the earth itself held a long sigh of relief. Behind closed eyes, I searched for my center, striving to decrypt the meanings woven through Mother Ayahuasca's teachings.

In the quiet depths of meditation, a subtle awareness washed over me. It was not only the inner peace that had settled within me; it was the serenity that extended throughout the entire space. I opened my eyes, surveying the scene around me. My brothers and sisters no longer writhed in pain, nor were they entangled in their struggles against inner darkness. The suffering that had once permeated the ceremony had dissipated, leaving a gentle tranquility in its wake.

The maloca, once brimming with energy and intensity, now radiated peace. My companions, who had battled their purges with fervor, rested quietly. Some reclined on their mats, lost in deep slumber, while others sat in tranquil stillness, their faces relaxed and their breaths deep and steady. There were no more weeping or desperate cries for assistance. Instead, an atmosphere of serene harmony prevailed, as if the collective weight of suffering had lifted and was replaced by the quiet resonance of healing.

The healing energy vibrated through the maloca's wood and thatch, surrounding me with an undeniable presence. This force exuded a warmth that penetrated my core, echoing something ancient and profound within me. The jungle's vibrancy and the earth's rhythmic pulse merged in our sacred sanctuary, flowing through each individual gathered there. Through my willing sacrifice and the deep purging I undertook for my kin, a healing portal had opened. Their pain, once prominent within me, now dissolved into the ether. In this moment of clarity, I grasped that the ceremony's true power transcended personal change; we were engaged in a collective metamorphosis.

My heart was filled with gratitude, a glow radiating from my very core. I saw each face around me, each soul on this sacred journey, and felt an overwhelming sense of unity. No longer were we isolated travelers on disparate paths; we were interlinked through something greater: a shared journey of healing and transformation. The love of the sacred space, the jungle, and the essence of

Mother Ayahuasca herself flowed through us, binding us in an unbreakable bond.

In the silence and tranquility, everything had transformed. The pain and suffering experienced during the ceremony served as gateways through which we had traversed, and on the other side, we had emerged stronger, lighter, and more interconnected. In this warmth of shared experience, I harbored deep gratitude for the ceremony, the teachings imparted, and the unconditional love binding us all. We had shared something extraordinary, something everlasting. This gift will remain with me forever.

As the ceremony drew to a close, the final notes of the shamans' icaros faded into the night, and the energy in the maloca transformed. The heavy burden of the ceremony and the intensity of the purging melted away into a gentle, soothing calm. The jungle outside, which had once echoed with fervent sounds, now softened, embodying the lessons learned throughout the night. The night air felt rejuvenated, fresh, and purified. I lay upon my mat, feeling the earth beneath me—solid and grounding—allowing myself to be enveloped in this serene atmosphere. The entire universe exhaled alongside me, releasing its tensions and finding solace within this sacred space.

I closed my eyes, surrendering to the stillness encircling me. My body, exhausted yet revitalized from the intense release, began to relax, and my mind eased, calming after the night's tumult. Gradually, I drifted into a profound slumber that was so pure and sacred that it felt like a return to a timeless healing energy. This sleep heralded rebirth, a complete rest that restored the core of my being and mended the fragments of my soul that the ceremony had torn asunder. In this dreamless state, a force far grander than I cradled me. The universe embraced me, allowing me to heal within its nurturing fold.

When dawn's light began to filter through the maloca's open walls, I awoke feeling transformed, as if my being had undergone thorough cleansing and renewal. The soft golden light filtering through the jungle canopy bore the warmth of a new day, infusing everything with vibrancy. The morning remained tranquil, the jungle's sounds subdued, as if even the trees and creatures granted this moment of reflection.

The curandera awaited our arrival, exuding a serene and nurturing aura. In her hands, she cradled a bowl filled with a sacred blend of flowers, meticulously prepared the night before with enchanted herbs and delicate petals. A rich aroma enveloped me, intoxicating my senses with the essence of jasmine and rose, along with a captivating earthy note that echoed the heartbeat of the jungle. As she poured the cool, fragrant water over me, I felt a profound sense of liberation. Every trace of the ceremony's intensity and lingering shadows was swept away. The petals clung to my skin, their fragrance surrounding me like a warm embrace. My spirit blossomed anew as I released the weight of sorrow, uncertainty, and attachment.

I remained for a moment, immersed in the beauty and strength of the ritual, absorbing the full significance of what had unfolded. My body felt light, almost ethereal, liberated from the weight of past experiences, leaving me clear, whole, and deeply connected to everything around me. The ceremony revealed the essence of healing, transcending individual understanding and transforming into a collective awakening. I felt the intricate web binding myself, the shamans, my spiritual brothers and sisters, the jungle, and the spirit of Mother Ayahuasca. Everything was interwoven, and I belonged within it all.

While my journey would extend far beyond this moment, a profound understanding had taken root within me. True healing emerged through surrender and sacrifice, and in our willingness to give of ourselves, we received the greatest gifts. The energy of interconnectedness unveiled throughout the ceremony formed a sacred bond among us all, transcending the physical realm and connecting us to the eternal. This gift would remain with me, not merely as a memory but as a living truth to embody as I moved forward.

Chapter Four

The Sacred Valley of Reflection

Following my initial retreat at Nimea Kaya Sanctuary, I chose not to return home immediately. A deep, instinctual resistance held me back from reentering the familiar world too soon. I felt an internal urgency to remain and reflect on the significant revelations I had just undergone. An unsettling sense of incompleteness compelled me to pause and allow the profound experiences to settle within me. The intensity of the ceremonies, the visions, and my encounters with Mother Ayahuasca had fundamentally altered my life, and I recognized the necessity of having the space to process it all.

I set off into the Sacred Valley, a land celebrated for both its stunning beauty and spiritual essence. Here, the whispers of ancient wisdom still resonate through the mountains and rivers. The Sacred Valley summoned me; its vibrant energy soothed the internal chaos I carried. With its timeless vistas and tranquil ambiance, the Valley offered a sanctuary for delving into the layers of my experiences.

As my journey unfolded, I became enthralled by the rich interplay of nature and history that characterizes the Sacred Valley. The majestic peaks of the Andes stood watch, draped in mist, protecting the lush landscape below. The crisp air, imbued with purity, combined with the dazzling colors of terraced fields and the rhythmic murmurs of flowing rivers, breathed life into the terrain. Each twist and turn revealed an unmistakable vitality; the land felt alive, sharing its stories of an ancient bond between humanity and the cosmos.

It was akin to entering a sacred haven where time slowed, and the distractions of the modern world faded into oblivion. Within the enduring wisdom of the Inca civilization, I sensed an opportunity to comprehend the revelations presented to me during the Ayahuasca ceremonies. Each step I took on this hallowed ground carried meaning, as if my journey were part of a broader unfolding narrative.

Upon reaching Ollantaytambo, a quaint town nestled alongside the Patakancha River, I was immediately enchanted by its ageless charm. It felt as though I had stepped into a portal leading to another epoch where history, nature, and spirituality thrived in unison. The town's cobbled streets meandered through ancient stone structures, and every turn revealed a new wonder. The air was infused with the essence of antiquity, each stone bearing witness to the wisdom of the ages.

The towering Inca terraces, skillfully carved into the hillside, stood as monumental sentinels of this sacred site. Their weather-beaten surfaces told tales of centuries past, while their intricate craftsmanship remained astonishing. Each stone fit together so perfectly that it was hard to discern where one ended and another began. These terraces, once remarkable feats of agricultural ingenuity and defensive strongholds, now served as silent witnesses to a legacy of resilience and creativity.

With each breath, the invigorating mountain air filled my lungs, grounding and energizing me in equal measure. Its earthy scent mingled with the freshness of the rushing river nearby. The sound of the Patakancha River cascading over smooth rocks echoed the whispers of history—a melody of continuity reminding me that life flows endlessly, linking generations and spirits.

The profound essence of the place permeated my being. The hills seemed animated with narratives, their rugged contours molded not just by human hands but by the relentless passage of time and nature. Ollantaytambo was more than a town; it was an organic connection to an ancient world. Every building, pathway, and eddy in the river felt like a fragment of a larger puzzle I was beginning to decipher. The land itself urged me to listen and to open my heart to the lessons trapped within its stones and waters.

I wandered within the Araqhama compound, where the past and present coexisted flawlessly. The painstakingly crafted stone walls emanated a quiet resilience, their surfaces seasoned yet steadfast. Each stone felt alive, murmuring tales of the hands that had placed it there with care, skill, and commitment. As I navigated through the compound, the atmosphere buzzed with a wordless reverence—a tacit respect for the sacred nature of this land.

Compelled by an invisible force, I ascended the hill of Cerro Bandolista, home to the Inca ceremonial center. Each step along the worn path felt sacred, the ground beneath my feet thick with the wisdom of an ancient civilization. The ascent was neither taxing nor effortless; it possessed intention. A powerful sense of unity with the energy of this space enveloped me as I followed in the footsteps of countless seekers before me.

Upon reaching the pinnacle, I was greeted by the terraces that rose magnificently—a stunning display of human ingenuity and spiritual commitment. They ascended gracefully, reaching for the heavens. Their design transcended mere functionality, embodying a poetic harmony that reflected a culture that saw no divide between the sacred and the mundane. These structures were not just agricultural terraces; they were altars to the cosmos, forging a connection between earthly existence and divine realms.

I halted, allowing the sheer magnitude of the scene to wash over me. The view was breathtaking; the Sacred Valley unfolded below like a grand, living tapestry. The meandering river sparkled in the sunlight, nourishing the land. The mountains loomed protectively, their peaks veiled in mist as if guarding the secrets of the ancients.

I felt an intimate connection with the people who constructed these marvels. Their relentless faith, precision, and knowledge of the universe echoed through every stone, terrace, and pathway. Their spirit lingered, intricately woven into the fabric of the land. I sensed their presence and wisdom, extending a reverence for life and the divine.

At that moment, I ceased to be merely a visitor. I became part of an eternal narrative—a mere thread in the vast tapestry of existence. The ceremonial center was more than a physical location; it represented a profound experience, a portal to comprehending the interconnectedness of all life. Within its silence, it conveyed profound truths. I stood in awe, humbled, and grateful for the opportunity to experience its energy.

From Ollantaytambo, my path led me toward Machu Picchu, often hailed as the crowning glory of the Inca Empire. The journey to the citadel represented both a physical and spiritual ascent, winding through lush forests and cliffs, each step drawing me closer to the heavens. When I finally arrived at the site, perched high on a mountain ridge nearly 8,000 feet above sea level, the sheer magnificence took my breath away.

The air was cool and invigorating, infused with the scents of earth and foliage, as clouds danced around the ancient stone edifices. The sky seemed to descend to touch this sacred ground, creating an ethereal aura that blurred the boundaries between heaven and earth. Sunlight filtered through the mist in golden beams, illuminating some terraces and temples while casting others in shadow. The delicate interplay of light and fog rendered the site dreamlike, transporting it to a realm beyond ordinary time.

As I stood among the ruins, I sensed a vibe of the eternal—an energy vibrating through the stones and reaching deep into my being. The terraces etched into the mountain stretched outward like colossal stairways toward the Divine, their meticulous design a testament to the Inca people's exceptional harmony with nature. The temples, adorned with intricate masonry and precisely aligned to celestial events, hummed with a quiet wisdom that spoke directly to my soul.

The energy engulfed me, transcending anything I had ever felt: subtle yet profound, gentle yet fierce. The essence of life and the interconnectedness of all beings resonated in the air. I closed my eyes and inhaled deeply, allowing the land's vibrations to resonate within me. Machu Picchu existed not just as a location but as a living, breathing entity—a bridge between the terrestrial and the Divine.

Gazing over the Sacred Valley from the heights of Machu Picchu stirred a deep sense of Oneness within me. The winding Urubamba River mirrored the flow of life itself—ever-changing, yet eternal. The towering mountains surrounding the citadel stood like ancient guardians, their presence both protective and awe-inspiring.

In this sacred place, I metamorphosed from a mere tourist into an integral part of something far greater. The terraces, temples, and mountains whispered age-old truths, reminding me of the intricate web of existence that binds us all. Immersed in the grandeur of Machu Picchu, I felt an overwhelming sense of gratitude and humility. The land invited me to remember, to reconnect, and to awaken to the sacredness present in all things.

Amidst the awe-inspiring beauty of the Sacred Valley, my mind raced, returning to the ceremonies at Nimea Kaya. Moments of intensity and revelation replayed vividly within me. The striking memory of the Serpent God, his gaze shimmering with ancient knowledge, remained alongside the tender yet transformative dialogues I had with Mother Ayahuasca. These recollections were not merely ephemeral insights but keys to a door I had yet to unlock ultimately.

The words spoken during those sacred moments, "You always wanted to know who you are. Now you know," resonated within me, hauntingly persistent. At that time, they struck me with such intensity that they laid my soul bare. Now, standing amidst the majestic Andes, those words took on new layers of mystery. What did they mean? Who was I? Was this identity something to rediscover, or had I always possessed it, just momentarily forgotten?

As I pondered, questions multiplied. What was the true meaning behind these experiences? Were they mere figments of an overactive imagination—visions birthed from the potent brew of Ayahuasca? Or were they glimpses into a deeper reality shrouded beyond the confines of the ordinary, awaiting my perception? The vividness of the ceremonies felt tangible. The visions were not dreams or fantasies but encounters with realms that were more authentic and vibrant than anything I had experienced in everyday life.

Within the ancient ruins of Machu Picchu, surrounded by extraordinary beauty, the connection between the sacred land and my internal exploration became unmistakable. The Inca people had constructed their temples and terraces in perfect harmony with the cosmos, honoring the unseen forces that govern existence. My visions at Nimea Kaya aligned with a cosmic truth greater than myself—an intimate yet boundless reality.

Lingering doubts accompanied me, as they often do during times of profound revelation. Were these experiences my mind's way of grappling with the incomprehensible, or was my mind merely a vessel interpreting a truth that transcended its capabilities? The Serpent God, Mother Ayahuasca, and the sacred teachings held such palpable reality that diminishing them to mere hallucinations would be both reductive and an affront to the sanctity of my experiences.

The reality I encountered during those ceremonies resonated with more authenticity than the world I now navigated. The colors glowed richer, the sensations gleamed deeper, and the emotions flowed unfiltered and raw. I had stepped into the very essence of existence, stripped of pretense, and glimpsed the profound truth of my being. In this Sacred Valley of the Incas, surrounded by their timeless legacy, I recognized an undeniable connection between their quest for divine comprehension and my own.

The energy of the Valley felt simultaneously grounding and expansive, inviting me to trust the unfolding of my discoveries. I recognized that I need not force an understanding of my retreat experiences; instead, I should allow the truth I had encountered to reveal itself in its rhythm, like a delicate flower unfolding. The Sacred Valley imparted wisdom—that some answers are not meant to be pursued but welcomed in stillness.

The words, "You always wanted to know who you are. Now you know," echoed once more, urging me to explore their true implications. Was I merely a witness to these transient experiences? Or was I the essence infused in the visions, the eternal consciousness that Mother Ayahuasca had illuminated? The answer would not surface through rationale or analysis; it would emerge through surrender, embracing the mystery without the urge to explain it.

The journey had only just begun. These inquiries, these fleeting moments of wonder and doubt, served not as obstacles but as vital stages. They led me toward a profound comprehension, drawing me nearer to the truth that had always lingered within me. As the sun sank behind the Andes, bathing the Sacred Valley in a golden embrace, I discovered a serene determination. The solutions would arrive not through spoken words or explanations but from the quiet awareness that emerges when we reclaim what has always been ours.

My intrigue intensified as I revisited the enigma of my Ōura ring. The vivid recollection of checking its readings before the ceremony lit my mind. It operated seamlessly, documenting each heartbeat and every movement with accuracy. After the ceremony, the data returned as expected—a smooth continuation of my vital signs. Yet during the sacred hours of the ceremony, the device recorded nothing: no heart rate, no breath count, no movement. A void existed where life should have manifested. For that fleeting moment, I had stepped beyond the realm of the living.

The implications overwhelmed me. Had I crossed into a dimension beyond the confines of physical reality? My rational mind struggled to comprehend this disparity. The ring captured the essence of life —the steady cadence of a heart, the rhythm of breath, the vitality of movement. Yet undeniable evidence showed a discrepancy, a silence as if my body had momentarily ceased to be during those hours. The empty space on the screen embodied something sacred—a testament to the profound mystery inherent in my experience.

This insight ignited a deluge of questions. What does it mean to "cross over"? Had I detached from my physical form, stepping into realms where our known existence vanished? The ceremonies throbbed with vivid reality; their sensations and sights were more striking than waking life itself. Perhaps, in those moments, I had touched something eternal—an existence beyond the limits of flesh and bone.

I recalled the moments during the ceremony when liberation enveloped me—weightless and formless, a pure essence suspended in an infinite expanse. This release transcended all I had previously known, loosening the physical world's hold and allowing me to unite with something vast and timeless. The absence of data on my ring confirmed this transformation. Beyond a symbolic death, I ventured into a realm that eluded measurement and merged into the Absolute.

These questions pursued and captivated me: was this evidence of a greater reality, an affirmation of the existence of dimensions beyond our perception? Or was it merely a technical glitch, a blip in the data? Deep within, I sensed that it was neither and yet something infinitely more profound. It was an invitation to acknowledge the dimensions of existence unrecorded by technology or science— realms that are felt and experienced rather than merely analyzed.

As I reflected, it became apparent that the ring's silence conveyed a message—a subtle affirmation from the universe that the experiences I encountered existed beyond the physical plane. They were real, not in terms of the tangible world, but in a way that transcended it. The absence of data was not a void but a fullness—a space where the infinite communicated its truths.

This revelation deepened my determination to explore further. I realized these questions demanded answers. The mysteries of my experience, the silence of my ring, and the profound revelations from the ceremonies beckoned me to return and delve into the realms I had merely begun to explore. Whatever awaited me, I felt assured it would not be defined by technology or empirical studies but through the depths of my soul.

I sensed that my journey remained unfinished. The Sacred Valley, with its ancient wisdom etched into every stone and carried on the gentle breezes, provided a refuge for reflection. Yet within its stillness, it stirred a longing—a deep hunger to probe more profoundly into the mysteries unfolding during my retreat. I had been entrusted with fragments of an extraordinary puzzle, each piece revealing a cosmic truth, though the complete image still eluded me.

The gazes of the Serpent God lingered vividly in my mind, commanding and brilliant as in the vision. His presence transcended an image, enveloping me in a potent energy that invited me to explore realms of understanding far beyond the tangible. The dialogue with Mother Ayahuasca echoed in my heart, her words overflowing with love, guidance, and universal insight. These experiences had not dulled with time; if anything, they intensified, urging me to interpret their meaning.

The visions revealed themselves not as random occurrences but as vibrant truths, alive and pulsating with significance. They seemed to whisper ancient wisdom, understood by my soul even when my mind struggled to catch up. The ethereal worlds glimpsed were not mere illusions but vibrant realms rich with purpose and wisdom, offering glimpses of something far grander than my individual being.

I understood that the truths imparted by Mother Ayahuasca were not answers but invitations—calls to venture deeper, to pose more significant questions, and to awaken to realities beyond the threshold of my understanding. "You always wanted to know who you are. Now you know," she stated. But had I truly? Her words served as both solace and disquiet—like a riddle pointing toward the infinite yet still just out of reach.

The Sacred Valley echoed these questions. The ancient stones of Ollantaytambo, the terraces of Machu Picchu, and the rivers winding through the mountains resonated with the same eternal energy felt during the ceremonies. It seemed the land, too, urged me to listen more attentively and feel more profoundly. The interconnectedness experienced during the ceremonies—being part of something vast and timeless—was mirrored in each sound, shadow, and gust of wind in the Sacred Valley.

I began to realize that my journey was not merely in pursuit of answers; it was about surrendering to the mystery itself. The visions, the Serpent God, and the wisdom of Mother Ayahuasca were guiding me toward a more profound and transformative experience. Answers would not arise from analysis or logical deduction; they would emerge through lived experiences and the willingness to step into the unknown once again.

As each day passed, my yearning intensified. I understood the Sacred Valley was a pause—a place to gather strength in preparation for the forthcoming journey. The pieces of the puzzle were not intended to be assembled here; they served as clues directing me back to the medicine, back to the ceremonies, and deep into the essence of who I am. The revelations glimpsed were merely the inception of a quest—an ember igniting a deeper pursuit of truth, healing, and understanding.

As my time in the Sacred Valley waned, I found myself suspended between two worlds, my heart pulled in divergent directions. On the one hand, I felt a growing readiness to embrace the familiarity of my life, while on the other, I grappled with reluctance to leave the profound energy of this sacred space. The Sacred Valley cradled me like a timeless guardian, its mountains watching over me and its rivers sharing age-old truths. The land thrummed with life, bestowing wisdom with each breath of wind and ray of sunlight, and I had only just begun to uncover its mysteries. The thought of departing before fully unearthing them left a hollow ache within me.

I meandered through the Valley one last time, absorbing the earthy aromas and vibrant flora, accompanied by the distant symphony of birds and the rhythmic flow of water against stone. Each element resonated with the experiences of the ceremonies, reinforcing the interconnected nature of existence. The air trembled with vitality, echoing within me. The Valley imparted a final lesson—a message I was not yet ready to grasp.

Doubt washed over me at the cusp of the journey. Had I overlooked something essential? Did the Sacred Valley harbor answers I had been too distracted to perceive? The mountains and rivers revealed themselves as educators, sharing the same essence as the Serpent God and Mother Ayahuasca, imparting a singular truth: the Divine is not separate from us, nor is it an endpoint. It breathes life into every stone, every droplet of water, and every inhalation we take.

The pull to return to the world beyond the Valley grew undeniable. The teachings of this sacred land would unveil themselves with time, surfacing in my awareness when least expected. Leaving the Valley did not equate to forsaking its wisdom. It would remain within me, intricately woven into the fabric of my existence, poised to guide me as I stepped back into the world with renewed eyes and an open heart.

The mountains stood resilient, their peaks caressed by dawn's golden light, while the rivers continued their unending journey. I silently expressed gratitude for this sacred land, knowing its energy and insight had merged with my being. Though I was stepping away, I carried the Valley inside—its whispers of truth and eternity echoing through my soul.

For two years after my initial retreat, these inquiries wove seamlessly into the fabric of my daily life. The vivid memories of the ceremonies remained etched in my mind. I revisited them daily, not as passing thoughts but as intentional reflections, scrutinizing every interaction with

Mother Ayahuasca, each vision of the Serpent God, and every profound insight that surged through me during those sacred nights. Each moment held deep significance, and I was resolute in my quest to unravel each layer to reveal the core of my experience.

The visceral sensations of the ceremonies lingered: the warmth of the maloca, the unforgettable beauty of the icaros, and the vibrant energy pulsating through me as visions unfolded. I beheld otherworldly realms with surreal clarity—more vivid than the physical world to which I awakened each day. The wisdom bestowed by Mother Ayahuasca resonated within me as an eternal refrain: "You always wanted to know who you are. Now you know." Her words transformed into a riddle I could not ignore. What did she mean? Who was I?

With each moment of reflection, these experiences reshaped how I perceived reality. They shattered the limitations of what I deemed possible, compelling me to confront truths that defied logic. I questioned everything I had once held as certainty. Was this world, with its tangible solidity, an elaborate illusion? Were the visions and divine encounters the true foundation of existence? The borders distinguishing the seen and unseen, the known and unknown, began to blur.

Amidst this introspection, the question persisted: "Who am I?" It transcended conventional notions of identity, moving beyond names and roles toward something more primal—the essence of existence itself. Was I merely an observer of these cosmic insights, or was I a vital part of them—a manifestation of the divine consciousness that

Mother Ayahuasca had unveiled? Was I merely a drop in the ocean, or was I the ocean itself?

Amidst a sea of profound questions and mystical experiences, one individual became my tether to reality: Dr. Vasile Munteanu. A philosophy professor who entered my life as if orchestrated by fate, he became the sole person with whom I could share these deep experiences without fear of judgment. His profound grasp of both Eastern and Western philosophical traditions granted him a unique perspective on my quest. Where others may have dismissed my experiences as fantasy, he listened intently, offering insights that helped me traverse the space between mystical realms and the tangible world I inhabited.

Dr. Munteanu emerged as more than a mentor; he transformed into a guiding light in my philosophical and spiritual inquiries. His unwavering support empowered me to pursue my academic aspirations while embracing these profound questions. His encouragement helped me strike a balance between the analytical rigor of academia and the profound mysteries uncovered during my spiritual encounters. My gratitude toward him transcends ordinary appreciation. Under his guidance, I learned that one could simultaneously embrace scholarly pursuits and spiritual exploration, recognizing that both are complementary paths to understanding the infinite complexity of existence.

It was this relentless pursuit—this insatiable thirst for understanding—that ultimately drew me back to Nimea Kaya. The questions that took root during my first retreat burgeoned, urging me to seek answers that could be found only in Mother

Ayahuasca's sacred realm. I recognized the necessity of returning, surrendering once more to the medicine, and diving deeper into the mysteries that had both enlightened and perplexed me. The experiences of my initial retreat provided glimpses of something extraordinary; however, those glimpses felt like an invitation—a door ajar—enticing me to step into its fullness.

The Sacred Valley had acted as a conduit between two realms. Its ancient ruins, towering mountains, and gently flowing rivers offered me the space to reflect and begin processing the profound revelations I encountered. Walking its storied paths, I felt like a pilgrim, preparing my heart and mind for what lay ahead. The Valley whispered its wisdom, reminding me that answers often emerge not from the clamor of searching but from the stillness of simply being. Yet, despite its beauty and tranquility, I recognized it was not my final destination; it was a waystation—an opportunity to gather resolve for the journey to come.

I carried the Sacred Valley's energy within me—a blend of serenity and determination, gratitude and anticipation. The landscapes I departed seemed to breathe as if the Valley itself understood the journey upon which I embarked and offered its blessings. The imposing mountains, with their eternal watchfulness, assured me that the truths I sought were as enduring as their presence. The unending rivers, flowing through time and space, reminded me that my journey was a vital component of something greater than myself.

I felt the Amazon calling me anew; its vast, untamed vibrancy urged my return to Nimea Kaya. The thick jungle, the rhythmic pulse of life, and the sacred sanctuary of the maloca transcended mere locations; they became realms where the veil between the sacred and the profane thinned and where the answers I sought might finally reveal themselves. I could almost hear the icaros weaving through my thoughts, their haunting melodies guiding me back toward the medicine and the divine wisdom it granted.

This time, my sense of purpose was renewed. The uncertainty and hesitation that clouded my first retreat had dissipated. In its place lay quiet determination. I was ready to confront whatever the medicine had to present, regardless of difficulty or profundity. I understood that answers wouldn't manifest as neat conclusions or simple definitions; they would arise as transformative experiences—profound revelations requiring the relinquishment of archaic modes of thinking and being.

The voyage back to the Amazon felt like a return to my essence. As the plane descended over the lush expanse of the jungle, my heart surged with emotion—both excitement and reverence intertwined. I was not merely returning to a place; I was returning to a state of openness, embracing the potential for transformation. The jungle, in its raw, untamed energy, welcomed me back—as if it had been anticipating this moment all along.

I was ready to dive into the depths of the unknown once again, surrendering to the wisdom of Mother Ayahuasca and eager to uncover the profound truths that awaited me in the heart of the Amazon. This time, I was not merely a traveler; I was a seeker on a sacred journey, committed to embracing everything that unfolded before me.

Chapter Five

A Night of Compassion

Two years had passed since my initial retreat at Nimea Kaya, and the call of Mother Ayahuasca reverberated profoundly within me, permeating the very essence of my being. This was no ephemeral recollection but a steadfast longing, a gentle yet undeniable call to return. The insights and transformations I had undergone lingered in my spirit, persistently murmuring that there was still more to unveil, more to mend, and more to comprehend. The journey within the maloca had etched itself indelibly upon my soul, and now, as I readied myself for this return, I felt that the next chapter was vital. A significant transformation had occurred within me, and I was poised to plunge deeper into the mysteries that had only begun to unravel.

The return enriched my journey. I joined a diverse group of seventeen individuals, each drawn to the hallowed place by a shared resonance yet pursuing distinct paths. Our assembly of seven men and ten women bore unique narratives, challenges, and aspirations. Some sought healing, others sought clarity, while many craved a more profound communion with the Divine. Despite our varied backgrounds and seemingly separate lives, a deep sense of unity blossomed. The Divine intertwined our destinies in this sacred setting, melding our quests into a collective pilgrimage.

Within the maloca, the atmosphere was electrified, with tangible energy crackling in the air. The weight of our hopes and fears coalesced, merging with the sanctity of our surroundings. Each participant's intentions intertwined, and while our journeys remained personal, the collective spirit united us in both comfort and humility. The maloca became a sanctuary for our souls. This holy place cradled us as we ventured into the unknown, confronting truths and facing our shadows.

The others sat in stillness, preparing themselves, the atmosphere thick with expectation. There was a collective sense of openness and vulnerability. We had come to surrender, to place our trust in the wisdom of Mother Ayahuasca, and to embrace transformation. The energy of our collective intentions suffused the air, and from my seat, I felt that this experience would transcend all prior ones. The maloca stood as a silent observer of our shared journey, a sacred space where our healing would take place and where the medicine would guide us toward the answers we had sought for countless lifetimes.

The inaugural ceremony of the retreat distinctly showcased its exceptional nature. An air of palpable tension enveloped us as the jungle outside throbbed with a mysterious resonance, each tree and creature seemingly suspended in anticipation. The breeze rustled through the foliage while distant birdsong echoed in the night, creating a timeless, sacred harmony. Within the maloca, vibrant energy surrounded us, the jungle poised for our next actions. The dancing candlelight cast elaborate shadows across the walls, cultivating an atmosphere of closeness and reverence as we gathered, quietly priming ourselves for the journey that lay ahead.

As I settled into the circle with my fellow travelers, I sensed the collective energy rising; each participant was eager for the metamorphosis they yearned for. I cradled my cup of Ayahuasca, acutely aware of its weight—both tangible and symbolic. The earthy, bitter liquid resided inside like a promise, and with a measured breath, I drank, yielding to the medicine and the unfolding process. There was no immediate surge of sensations, no instant visions—merely a gentle settling of energy enveloping me. I leaned back, closed my eyes, and listened, allowing the sounds of the jungle to intermingle with the soft chants of the shamans.

Time felt distorted, unnervingly slow, yet still—there was no change. I sensed no shift in my awareness, nor did any profound insights emerge. The environment around me remained static, firmly rooted in the physical world, while my restless mind, always seeking significance, began to fill with uncertainty. A subtle wave of frustration surfaced as I wondered if Mother Ayahuasca had chosen to elude my perception that night. I wrestled with an odd blend of longing and confusion. There were no visions, no sacred encounters—just my quiet anticipation for an event that had yet to manifest. Understanding eluded me, and for a fleeting instant, I questioned whether I had overlooked a vital detail or failed to find the correct passage.

Deep within, I understood that this stillness held purpose; the absence of the expected rush of visions bore significance. I reminded myself that Mother Ayahuasca could not be hurried; she revealed herself in her own time, and at times, her silence carried more weight than any vision. Although I wasn't receiving what I had anticipated, I recognized the wisdom inherent in this waiting. The lack of visions felt like a lesson in patience, an invitation to surrender. I remained there quietly, releasing any expectations and opening myself to whatever would emerge, trusting that Mother Ayahuasca, in her profound way, was preparing me for something far beyond my immediate comprehension.

Motivated to delve deeper, I requested a second cup of Ayahuasca. The bitterness grazed my tongue once again, oddly soothing, as if it were preparing me for something both unfamiliar and known. I swallowed the contents without hesitation, hoping that this time, the medicine would unlock new revelations. As anticipation loomed, I remained buoyed in that state of stillness, my mind fidgety yet placid. The sound of icaros filled the air, occasionally punctuated by the gasps and groans of my spiritual brothers and sisters, melding with the mystical symphony of the jungle.

As minutes passed, the surrounding atmosphere thickened. I sensed energy shifting, the tension in the room palpable, yet nothing had transformed within me. Then, a voice from across the room captured my attention. It was a seemingly trivial remark but struck me as profoundly humorous in that moment. Laughter erupted from deep within, spilling forth until it became uncontrollable; I could hardly acknowledge the absurdity around me—the moans of participants invoking profound releases transformed into a source of unreserved amusement. Giggles flowed seamlessly through me.

For an ephemeral moment, I surrendered to the ludicrousness of it all. I mused, "Well, perhaps tonight will be amusing. Let's enjoy the show!" The laughter liberatingly diffused the weight I had been carrying. It was an unexpected twist, veering away from the solemnity I had anticipated, yet it reminded me of the lightness that Mother Ayahuasca could instill. Amid the potent healing unfolding around me, she allowed space for joy, playful acknowledgment, and the understanding that not every moment required somber seriousness. I felt genuinely present, unfettered by expectations, simply absorbing the experience as it unfolded in all its surprising and often amusing intricacies.

Just as I began to dissolve into the playful energy of the moment, an unexpected jolt shattered my laughter. Without forewarning, a gentle yet undeniable force tugged at my right ear, tilting my head to one side. An unseen hand guided me, steering my focus with subtle firmness. The shift was immediate; the joy faded, replaced by a deepening intensity as if the heartfelt energy demanded my full attention.

Suddenly, like a wave of insight, the voice of Mother Ayahuasca emerged, crystal clear yet imbued with tenderness and authority. "Be kind!" she urged, her words resonating deep within. The tone was not harsh but compelling—a loving reminder that every soul present was navigating their struggles. "Everyone is going through a rough time. Send them your love!" Her request wrapped around me, weighing heavily on my heart.

I felt the urgency of her message immediately, transforming my energy from lightness to deep empathy. The levity that had colored my perception now appeared as a distraction, a curtain shrouding the sacred work at hand. The laughter had been a release, indeed, but I understood that the true essence of this experience lay in extending compassion and being present amidst the suffering of my companions. The pull on my ear was not a reprimand but a soft nudge toward a deeper understanding—an invitation to honor the sacred nature of each person's journey and to offer my full support.

My once playful mind has now shifted to a state of serene respect. I settled into the stillness, embracing the weight of Mother Ayahuasca's message. Laughter receded, replaced by an emerging wellspring of compassion. I straightened my posture, recognizing that this night transcended personal entertainment; it was a call to serve. The air became charged with anguish, pressing heavily as the collective suffering of my fellow participants felt tangible, echoing against the maloca's walls. I closed my eyes and began to send love, envisioning golden light emanating from my heart and wrapping around each individual in warmth and solace. The act of giving emerged as healing, an expression of a language I had longed to speak. The frivolity dissipated, revealing the profound truth that the essence of this journey lay in connection, love, and the shared humanity that binds us all.

The atmosphere within the maloca constricted around me, heavy with an intricate tapestry of emotions. I felt drawn to the outdoors, longing to breathe in the night air. I stepped quietly to the exit, immersing myself in the jungle's darkness. The scene before me was breathtaking.

Above me sprawled an infinite expanse; the night sky was a profound canvas of deep navy adorned with countless stars. Each star shimmered like a crystalline pinprick against the darkness, forming constellations that danced to their singular rhythm and whispered tales of bygone eras. The Milky Way spiraled gracefully, a luminous river of starlight traversing the cosmos. Standing beneath this grandeur, I felt simultaneously minuscule and interconnected with the cosmic ballet unfolding above.

Life pulsed through the surrounding jungle with an ineffable vitality, creating a concerto of nocturnal sounds. The foliage whispered cryptic messages while insects harmonized in perfect rhythm with nature's melody. The rich, loamy scents blended with the jungle's vibrant energy, mingling with an aura that was mystical and transcendent.

The enormity of existence enveloped me as I stood still beneath the heavens. I realized that Mother Ayahuasca's gifts transcended personal journeys and visions. Sometimes, her magic resided in pure presence—immersing oneself in reality and attuning to the universal rhythms that intertwined with my heartbeat. A serene tranquility filled the night, and in that stillness, I sensed my unity with all existence: the stars above, the soil beneath, the surrounding forest, and the pure awareness permeating everything.

The pull of the ceremony eventually guided me back inside. The atmosphere within the maloca had shifted, yet it retained its powerful resonance. The shamans harmonized effortlessly, their sacred icaros weaving through the darkness and crafting protective pathways for our spiritual exploration. Their voices anchored us as Mother Ayahuasca began to unveil her mysteries.

Upon returning to my place, I aligned myself with the flow of the ceremony. My heart expanded in solidarity with my brothers and sisters, radiating warmth and understanding. I dedicated myself to supporting their journeys, offering silent strength. Every inhalation felt like a gift; every exhalation was a heartfelt wish for their healing. I witnessed their journeys—their moments of release and their cries of difficulty—not as an outsider but as a contributor to their spiritual growth. My purpose that night became clear: to hold sacred space for others, to experience their challenges as my own, and to understand that this act of service was my calling.

As the ceremony progressed, I stood steadfast as a silent sentinel, watching over my brothers and sisters. There was no need for words or gestures, only the profound, resolute knowledge that this was my role. The maloca, alive with energy and spirit, became a sanctuary where all raw, unspoken emotions were allowed to rise and be released. In that sanctuary, I offered my presence and support, encapsulating the energy of love as they confronted their healing. I felt no need for comprehension, only the necessity to remain fully present and surrender to the night's sacred essence.

As the ceremony drew to a close, a deep sense of fulfillment emerged within me. There were no monumental insights or blinding truths that altered reality; instead, a serene tranquility enveloped me. I stood by my brothers and sisters, witnessing their struggles and offering support within my means. In the stillness that followed, I recognized that the meaning of the evening was different; it was a deliberate act of giving, creating space for others, sharing compassion, and simply being present.

The humbling truth solidified in my heart: healing does not always manifest through grand insights or mystical experiences. Sometimes, it emerges from the quiet, humble act of standing alongside those who suffer, offering support without expectation. The power of healing rests in acts of compassion and in holding space for others to process, purge, and mend. There exists a sacred strength in merely being present, in sharing burdens, and in offering our love without a desire for reward. It serves as a reminder that, often, profound transformation unfolds not within ourselves but through the ways we uplift others.

The jungle's nighttime orchestral masterpiece lulled me into a profound sleep, its wild melodies threading through my awareness. Nature's chorus—the chirps of crickets and the distant calls of unseen wildlife—formed an ancestral lullaby that quieted my restless mind. Sleep transported me beyond the grasp of ordinary dreams to a realm where time flowed languorously, stretching and melding with infinity. The earth cradled me in its serene embrace while the forest stood vigilant, guarding my restoration. Here, my soul found the space to exist, revive, and simply be.

As dawn approached, a golden light flowed through the trees, drenching the maloca and gently awakening me from my repose. The curandera, exuding grace, moved purposefully to prepare the sacred floral bath. In her basin lay water steeped overnight with flowers and leaves, holding a profound stillness as if cradling the essence of the forest. Once poured over my head, the cool water cascaded down my skin, and the petals caressed me like delicate, loving hands, imbuing me with their blessings. Instantly, I sensed a transformation, a revitalization coursing through me, as if the energy of the plants traversed my being, dispelling any lingering shadows from the ceremony.

Although the ceremony had not yielded grand visions or otherworldly encounters, the internal metamorphosis I experienced was palpable. A sense of tranquility engulfed my heart, with a quiet understanding resonating deep within. The absence of extraordinary revelations made the experience all the more meaningful, revealing that spiritual growth does not solely arise from visions or profound insights; sometimes, it flourishes in the simplicity of presence and in the act of extending compassion without expectation.

A profound sense of gratitude welled within me, a deep acknowledgment of the truth that had permeated my heart. The experience reminded me that healing isn't always accompanied by grand moments of personal growth; often, it is about the quiet solidity of standing beside others, offering compassion, and being present in their journeys. Mother Ayahuasca helped me understand that this, too, embodies enlightenment—a way of navigating the world that prioritizes love and understanding for those around us. As I stood, bathed in the light of the new day, I felt rejuvenated and ready to carry this wisdom forward into the life that lay ahead.

Chapter Six

The Cosmic Classroom

The second ceremony of my retreat exuded a remarkably distinct energy. The maloca stood as a sacred vessel, embodying our collective intentions within a divine space. Flickering candles projected shadows across the walls while the sounds of the jungle outside intertwined seamlessly with the rhythm of my heartbeat. The atmosphere was serene, saturated with the expectation of a significant event about to unfold. As I sipped the Ayahuasca brew, the dense, earthy concoction grounded me, anchoring me firmly in the moment. I closed my eyes, allowing the weight of my intentions to permeate my very being.

With time, a gentle transformation began. Initially subtle and nearly undetectable, a delicate wave of energy coursed through me, awakening something resonant deep inside. As the brew settled within, I sensed the veil demarcating this world from the next beginning to dissolve. My senses sharpened, and every sound in the maloca—the distant calls of the jungle beings and the soft chants of the shamans—took on a richer significance. The jungle transformed into a living entity, intimate and inviting, as if the heart of awareness reached out to me, encouraging me to delve deep and experience the hidden breaths of existence.

As the ceremony unfolded, the linear flow of time disintegrated. My sense of self began to dissolve, suspending me in a boundless expanse. I felt myself expanding beyond the confines of my physical form. The boundaries of my existence faded, and I recognized the Oneness of the greater whole. Questions surrounding the nature of reality shifted from mere intellectual curiosity to visceral experience. The universe seemed to unfurl before me, revealing its intricate layers and complexities. Everything was interwoven: each thought, each atom, and every star. I ceased to be an observer and immersed myself fully in the universal interplay.

The energy within the maloca amplified as I opened myself to the unfolding experience. Mother Ayahuasca's voice resonated in my mind—calm yet insistent—guiding me through the revelations ahead. With every moment, I ventured further into the unknown, unraveling mysteries that had long eluded my intellect. The vastness of the universe, once perceived as an abstract outside reality, emerged as a manifestation within the infinite consciousness. This profound awakening illuminated the essence of existence: not as an isolated construct but as a reflection of pure awareness, in which all forms and experiences arise as manifestations. The truths I had sought were not distant revelations but intrinsic parts of my being. I realized the universe's secrets were meant to be experienced, lived, and embodied.

When the visions materialized, I was transported to a surreal dimension resembling a fusion of a classroom and a laboratory. The room carried an air infused with tangible energy that made every surface vibrate in resonance. As the space defined itself, Mother Ayahuasca's presence filled the room anew, distinctly different from my previous experiences. The comforting spirit I once felt had transformed into a commanding force, demanding reverence.

Her energy radiated with such potency that it coursed through my veins, making me acutely aware of her presence. There was no trace of gentleness in her gaze—only a piercing intensity that anchored me to the spot, rendering me unable to move. The atmosphere thickened with her formidable presence, transforming the space into a stage set for a confrontation that would shake me to my core. I entered this ceremony with the intention of understanding the nature of reality, seeking to unravel the mysteries of the universe.

Mother Ayahuasca, aware of my intentions, was not pleased. Her tone, unmistakably upset, echoed in my soul as she spoke, resonating not only in my ears but also deep within my very essence. "How dare you presume that reading a few physics textbooks will allow you to understand my greatness?" she thundered. Her words were more than merely spoken; they surged through me like a mighty wave, shifting my internal landscape and challenging the very foundation of what I believed I knew.

The weight of her indignation was overwhelming, piercing through my ego and illuminating the futility of my human efforts to grasp the universe's mysteries. My intellectual pursuit, grounded in logic and structured frameworks, seemed insignificant compared to the vast, boundless existence she embodied. I felt the righteous fire of her words penetrating the layers of arrogance within me, exposing the limits of my understanding. Her voice, reverberating through the space, was not just sound—it was pure energy, a current demanding humility. Each word she spoke stripped away the veil of certainty, leaving me with the humbling realization that there was so much more to life than I could ever conceptualize.

As the resonance of her words echoed in the very fabric of reality, I found myself breathless, confronting the realization that no amount of intellectual knowledge could ever fully capture the true essence of existence. I had attempted to dissect and comprehend its workings, but this was not a puzzle to solve; it was an experience to embrace—a force to feel. The realm of concepts, formulas, and theories felt achingly distant, leaving me within a profound silence, a deeper knowing accessible only to the heart. Her fury was not directed solely at me; it expanded outward, enveloping humanity's hubris —the folly of believing that the infinitely complex nature of reality could be quantified through mere equations and theories. The energy in the room escalated as if the fabric of reality responded to her righteous outrage.

Suddenly, a stack of my business cards materialized, floating into view as if summoned by her will. They seemed trivial, mere slips of paper bearing my name and title, overshadowed by the cosmic energy before me. With a swift gesture, she scattered them onto the ground. The cards fluttered away like forgotten remnants of a world that no longer mattered in the grand tapestry of existence. This act was symbolic, dismantling the illusion of control that humanity frequently clings to, reminding me that no title or achievement could genuinely convey our connection to the boundless consciousness.

As the cards lay abandoned, I felt the impact of that gesture resounding within me. What had once seemed vital—my carefully curated identity and intellectual pursuits—was stripped down to mere fragments, inconsequential in the face of a power far beyond human comprehension. She urged me, along with all of humanity, to relinquish the illusion of control and the pretense of wielding the universe. Those business cards, once emblems of my worldly identity, now represented the fragile constructs of a mind that had lost sight of consciousness's vastness.

"Your Ph.D. is meaningless," she proclaimed, her voice cracking through me like thunder. "Understand this: you are a warrior. You have always been and forever will be a warrior." Her words pierced deeply, akin to an arrow striking true. Their weight left me gasping as a profound humility washed over me. All the accolades, the recognition, and the intellectual achievements I had so fiercely amassed faded into nothingness. Years spent chasing knowledge in an attempt to understand the universe transformed into distractions from a far more profound truth. The hubris of assuming that my education could make me worthy of unveiling existence's mysteries became laughable, comparable to a child playing with toys in a world that demanded maturity and reverence.

An uncomfortable guilt welled within me, and for a fleeting moment, I yearned to shrink away from her piercing gaze. No longer an intellectual or a researcher, I felt more like a child in the presence of something vastly more significant. Yet, as her energy surrounded me, I sensed an alteration. Her fierce presence softened. The voice, once steeped in cosmic gravitas, turned warmer, infused with compassion. "But I know your heart," she said, a gentle reassurance lacing her words. "So, I will show you."

In those moments, I recognized a deep-seated truth within me, obscured by layers of learned concepts and pride. It wasn't about degrees or accolades; it transcended mere knowledge accumulation. This was a more profound calling, a purpose surpassing any academic pursuit. I understood that my quest had been misguided, searching for answers in the wrong places. Mother Ayahuasca now offered something more profound: a direct experience, a connection to the essence of existence.

Her words felt like a benediction, assuring me that the wisdom I sought would not reside in textbooks but within the experiences of life itself. It lived in surrender, humility, and acceptance of our grand interconnectedness. The weight of this realization settled within me, and with it came a newfound sense of peace. Mother Ayahuasca, in all her grace, was guiding me away from the intellectual arrogance of my past, leading me toward an understanding attainable only through the heart.

Unexpectedly, I found myself within a magnificent, otherworldly spaceship, an exquisite design that defied human imagination. Its surfaces glimmered with an ethereal luster, reflecting a light radiating from a central dome that filled the space with a serene yet electrifying energy. Surrounding me were intricate panels adorned with symbols and flickering multicolored lights, pulsating with a rhythm I struggled to grasp.

Drawn toward the core of the ship, where the dome beckoned, I found myself lying on an invisible table that materialized beneath me. Immobilized, panic momentarily threatened to overwhelm me. As I absorbed the sensation, any sense of danger evaporated, replaced by a profound uncertainty. My senses sharpened, attuned to a surge of unimaginable energy enveloping every cell of my body.

The energy felt like the very fabric of the universe merging with my essence. Each pulse charged me with a power so vast that it hinted at fundamental truths waiting to be unlocked. There was no pain—only exhilarating readiness. The energy flowed through me, invigorating every atom with purpose. It was as if I had been granted access to experience a moment far beyond ordinary human existence—a spiritual awakening, a metamorphosis at the foundational level.

As this energy intensified, I felt an undeniable connection to all that surrounded me. The ship, the light, and the expanse embraced me, and I belonged to it as it belonged to me. There was no division—only a fluid interchange of energy, intertwining everything in a harmonious dance. I inherently knew I was prepared for what lay ahead, curated for this precise moment. The swirling energy embraced me, revealing that I was part of an existence greater than comprehension.

Somehow, I knew that the robust energy coursing through me was not random; it had a profound purpose, preparing me for a monumental shift in perception that I could not yet comprehend. As Mother Ayahuasca moved gracefully within the glowing dome, I remained outside in the hallway of the spaceship, watching from a distance. She gathered the surrounding energy effortlessly, shaping it with clear intention; her movements were fluid and otherworldly. The light surrounding her radiated the very essence of creation, a brilliant energy that seemed to transcend space and time. The air around me pulsed with a thrilling intensity, and an overwhelming sense of expectation wrapped around me as though the cosmos itself paused, ready to unveil a long-anticipated moment.

I watched her with rapt fascination as she began to draw forth forms from the void—vast, luminous bursts that emerged into existence, sculpting the universe before my very eyes. These luminous expansions unfolded like the delicate petals of a divine bloom, emerging with a quiet yet undeniable force. Each burst seemed to encapsulate the seeds of a new reality, a fresh manifestation birthed with every expansion. It was a breathtaking display—a cosmic choreography of creation and dissolution unfolding simultaneously. The beauty overwhelmed me, each moment extending into eternity, ablaze with colors and light, harboring the mysteries of existence within their folds.

In that timeless state, my mind could only relate to the scene through the metaphor of radiant blossoms—intricate and delicate. The energy emanating from these forms was palpable, saturating the space with sacredness. Time was an irrelevant concept now—only an endless unfolding of light and form; the universe reconstituted itself before me. Yet, amidst the splendor and marvel, comprehension eluded me. The experience transcended intellectual processing—a pure, unfiltered wonder that imbued my being.

Only in retrospect did I comprehend the meaning of what I had watched: the blossoms I saw were, in fact, Calabi-Yau manifolds—complex shapes defining the hidden dimensions of String theory. Though I lacked the scientific framework to grasp these concepts initially, the connection between my visions and advanced theoretical physics concepts solidified vividly later. Despite my limited awareness, the experience imparted fundamental revelations, unveiling an intricate, interconnected tapestry of reality that surpassed my narrow human understanding.

I stood in awe, my senses overwhelmed by the extraordinary beauty unfolding before me. Each moment felt like a stroke of genius on a canvas too immense for my intellect to appreciate fully. The vibrant energy of the cosmos enveloped me, surging with vitality. Even amid this intensity, my mind grappled with categorization, attempting to comprehend the unfathomable—the experience aimed to transcend understanding, manifesting as pure, unmediated wonder.

"Please show me more," I whispered, a deep yearning in my voice. Mother Ayahuasca responded immediately, guiding me back to the charging table. Once again, a surge of cosmic energy flooded my being, awakening every cell in my body as the essence of existence flowed through me. This primeval energy coursed through my spirit, recalibrating my awareness. After this sacred calibration, I found myself once more amidst the translucent dome, poised to witness the unfolding mysteries within its holy confines.

Without hesitation, she began to create anew. This time, the world she birthed was even more intricate —each detail more vivid and harmonious as every element coalesced beautifully within it. Colors spiraled into a symphony; shapes expanded, and intricate designs emerged—a living universe coming alive, infused with energy and purpose. Its immensity inspired profound wonder, rendering me both small and intimately connected to its entirety.

This cycle of creation repeated itself multiple times, each iteration becoming more elaborate and expansive—a testament to the wonder of existence. I beheld a cosmic orchestral composition unfolding, with each new world echoing a fresh movement in a divine opus. Layers of reality magnificently shifted, with each creation woven into an ever-expanding fabric of existence. I engaged wholeheartedly in this sacred manifestation—awestruck and humbled in the face of its grandeur. This experience transcended ordinary time and space, affirming that I was integral to something infinitely greater than I had believed.

When the unfolding concluded, I experienced a curiously weighted blend of exhaustion and wonder. The sheer intensity of my revelations left me spellbound, struggling to process the enormity of what I had witnessed. The worlds, the exquisite designs, the energy—it all felt so expansive and intricate, and I had merely glimpsed the mechanics of existence. My body grew heavy, drained from the cosmic manifestations I had encountered, yet within that fatigue lay a fulfilling resonance born from profound revelations.

In an unexpected moment, Mother Ayahuasca returned. Her energy was serene yet assertive, and her words pierced my soul with weighty clarity. "Remember these truths," she began, her voice steady and unwavering: "Hinduism is the only true religion." The statement struck me like a bolt of lightning. "Not because the others are flawed," she elaborated, "but because of their incompleteness and the distortions that have occurred over time to serve different purposes."

Her words struck a chord within me, momentarily freezing my thoughts. This was not simply a religious directive; it was an insight into a truth that surpassed the confines of human belief. Her voice exuded confidence, devoid of judgment, revealing an essential reality obscured by layers of misconceptions. The profound nature of this realization left me astonished, compelling me to reevaluate everything I had understood about spirituality and faith.

She transitioned the discussion with a playful lightness in her voice. "String theory serves as the scientific framework for understanding reality. However, good luck uncovering the definitive solution," she said, with a hint of humor in her tone. I felt a subtle change in the air as she spoke, and an understanding began to form within me. The truth she was hinting at struck me: there were not just a few solutions to the puzzle of understanding the workings of the universe, but an unfathomable number—at least 10 to the power of 500. The realization that the key to unlocking the mysteries of existence was tantalizingly close yet eternally out of reach filled me with both wonder and intrigue. The lightness in her voice reminded me that, no matter how vast the knowledge we seek, the pursuit of truth must always be tempered by humility.

Finally, she disclosed something that sent a jolt of acknowledgment through me—an intimacy so unexpected that I struggled to breathe. "Katherine is Kali," she stated, alluding to my ex-wife, her voice steadfast and assured. A rush of understanding washed over me, a realization I had sensed but never articulated. "And your daughter," she continued gently, "is your mother." This revelation landed heavily in my chest, unfolding in layers as I attempted to reconcile the depth of this insight with my existing beliefs. It transcended mere familial ties; it illuminated a profound cosmic truth about the roles we inhabit in one another's lives. My mind spun as I endeavored to grasp the far-reaching implications of her words.

I remained speechless, grappling with the weight of these revelations. The evening's intensity enveloped me, my mind racing to catch up with the extraordinary events that had just transpired. The energy I had felt coursing through me, the shifts, the spiritual insights they coalesced into a tapestry that was both exquisite and bewildering. As my heart raced, I struggled to comprehend the situation, yet her words struck a profound chord within me, resounding through the core of my being.

Having consumed two cups of Ayahuasca that night, accompanied by an additional two unaltered cups from the previous ceremony, I suddenly realized how crucial this was. The quantity I ingested far exceeded that of many others present, and I began to understand why. Mother Ayahuasca revealed that this dosage was essential for me to withstand and decipher the intensity of my experiences. My journey was not merely a pursuit of insight or gentle visions; it was one of profound metamorphosis, requiring a larger quantity to accommodate its vastness. This was not just a spiritual undertaking; it was a deep initiation, demanding that I confront monumental truths about myself, the universe, and the interdependence of all existence.

At the beginning of the ceremony, I wore a crucifix around my neck—a symbol of faith and a source of comfort amidst the chaotic energy surrounding me. Just before the ceremony began, an incessant thought kept urging me to remove the crucifix from around my neck. At first, I resisted, unsure why I felt compelled to act against something so familiar and comforting. As this urge grew stronger, I complied without hesitation, removing the crucifix and setting it aside.

Mother Ayahuasca later revealed that the act wasn't about the crucifix's value or meaning but about shedding external influences that could hinder the messages she intended to impart. The ceremony required my complete openness, free from attachments or symbols that might cloud my perception. The crucifix, tied to a specific belief, represented a limitation—one that prevented me from fully embracing the limitless journey ahead. By letting go of this symbol, I allowed myself to be present in the moment, fully receptive to the teachings and experiences that Mother Ayahuasca had prepared for me.

This act involved more than merely discarding a physical object; it demanded that I relinquish my attachments. Mother Ayahuasca required me to abandon the comforting symbols of my former self, enabling me to fully absorb the revelations she wished to share. The messages she intended to communicate could not pass through the filter of old teachings, doctrines, or ingrained notions. She sought an empty vessel in me—one receptive to the emerging truths. I realized the profound significance of her request: it transcended the crucifix itself, encapsulating what it represented—the constraints of the ego and the mind's clinging to past identities and beliefs. By removing it, I began the journey toward true spiritual awakening.

As I lay on my mat, I struggled to digest the tumult of emotions and experiences from the past few hours. The visions, the intense sense of interconnectedness, and the cosmic insights swirled within me, making it challenging to reconcile them with my prior reality. The energy within the maloca vibrated around me, and the weight of the ceremony lingered in the air. Though my body felt weary and heavy, my mind was alert, striving to make sense of the divine revelations I had just encountered.

While lying there, attempting to steady my breath, I noticed a commotion out of the corner of my eye. A participant from India, a man I had briefly encountered before, was situated nearby. He emitted strange, disconcerting sounds, and his body contorted in unsettling ways. His movements were uncoordinated and erratic, far removed from the ordinary. He seemed to rise from the mat only to crash back down, his body caught in an unrelenting and forceful rhythm. It appeared as though an unseen force was manipulating him, exerting control over his actions.

He leaned forward and began to retch, yet there was something peculiar about it. He seemed to struggle against an obstruction as if something were lodged in his throat. The guttural noises escaping him reverberated through the maloca, sending chills down my spine. Anxiety crept back into my mind, forcing a question I hadn't intended to ask: Could this individual embody darkness? This thought pierced my consciousness uninvited, unsettling me profoundly as I pondered whether I was witnessing something sinister.

At that moment, Mother Ayahuasca's authoritative voice surged through my mind—fierce and penetrating. "How dare you think that way?" she reprimanded me, her tone radiating a powerful energy that coursed through my being. Her words left me breathless. "Do you know who this man is?" she inquired, and a wave of guilt flooded over me for harboring such a thought. "No," I confessed, my voice barely audible in the maloca's vast silence. Shame permeated me as I recognized my propensity to leap to conclusions, labeling the unfamiliar without due consideration.

"He embodies a noble soul," Mother Ayahuasca said, her tone gentle yet firm. "He chose to enter this world to transform negative energy into positive energy." Her words cut through my confusion with striking clarity. She was not merely recounting the man's behavior; she was revealing his intent. The concept of change, of converting darkness into light, struck a deep chord within me. His turmoil, his erratic movements, and his unease were not signs of malevolence but rather markers of significant spiritual labor that warranted both admiration and understanding.

"The collective purpose here," she elaborated, "is to witness this once-in-a-lifetime event." Her statement underscored the notion that this ritual transcended individual experiences; it connected to something primal and sacred. This was an extraordinary moment—one that would not arise again in many lifetimes—and we had gathered to observe the transformation, to learn from it, and to partake in an experience far greater than ourselves. The anguish I had previously felt began to diminish as the full weight of her explanation settled within me, leaving behind only a profound sense of awe and reverence for the sacred process unfolding before us.

She elaborated that the men in our circle were warriors, handpicked and trained by me in prior lives, tasked with safeguarding this revered individual and the women whom she referred to as goddesses. This was the true nature of the gathering, even if they were not aware of it. Among them was a high-ranking goddess, a realization that filled me with deep respect.

Receiving sacred teachings from Mother Ayahuasca profoundly touched me, evoking both holiness and humility. I was instructed to bow each time the shamans initiated their icaros, honoring not only the spiritual significance of the songs but also a being whose essence transcended the role of a mere participant in the ceremony. This dignified figure was my mentor from past lives. In those earlier times, I gained invaluable insights and guidance that surpassed the confines of time and space. It became evident that this soul had significantly influenced my spiritual journey; it was now my privilege and duty to honor him in the present.

With sincere reverence, I moved closer to him. Each step felt intentional, as if I were traversing sacred terrain. Upon reaching him, I knelt in a deep bow, overwhelmed by the realization of our profound connection. This act signified not only respect but also a silent tribute to the wisdom and experiences we had shared across many lifetimes. Memories flooded my mind—distant lessons and challenges that had culminated in this pivotal moment.

In that space of reverence, I spoke softly, my voice barely above a whisper but imbued with sincerity. "Let it out, master," I urged, my tone layered with compassion. "Let it out." There was an urgent warmth in my voice. I sensed the weight of his release: decades of pain, fear, and darkness he had carried. Feeling the depth of his transition, I wanted to provide the support, love, and space necessary for him to let go.

This was not merely encouragement; it was an invitation to surrender to the transformation we were all experiencing in that sacred setting. I wanted him to feel accompanied and recognized by our collective presence, just as he had guided me in previous lives. Standing there and witnessing his journey, an intense sense of connection washed over me, reminding me of our unity—that joy, pain, and release were intricately woven into the divine tapestry. My words transformed into a quiet prayer of healing and love, urging him to disentangle himself from what needed to be released, thereby opening pathways for a renewed sense of freedom.

The words of Mother Ayahuasca echoed in my mind: "El sueño de la razón produce monstruos." She urged me to vocalize it, and as I did, my voice infused the sacred atmosphere of the maloca with profound meaning. The phrase reverberated powerfully, haunting yet liberating, enveloping not just my spirit but everyone gathered in the ceremony. At that moment, I grasped that this message reached beyond my awareness and was meant to resonate with the entire group. It served as a poignant reminder that we frequently allow our rational minds to overshadow the intuitive, deeper essence of who we are.

The thought that unrestrained reasoning could conjure up monsters—representing our fears, regrets, or skewed perceptions—struck a profound chord within me. This realization extended beyond my individual experience; it was a shared awakening. By stifling our instinctual selves, we nurture these "monsters," allowing them to proliferate and influence our realities, erecting barriers to growth, peace, and genuine understanding.

As Mother Ayahuasca encouraged forgiveness, I felt an overwhelming urgency to atone for the wrongs I had committed, particularly toward the women in my life. The weight of past mistakes, especially the times when women had not been treated with the respect they deserved, grew too heavy to carry. It seemed as though this message reached beyond my own experiences—a call for all men to recognize the pain caused by centuries of mistreatment of women. With humility, I spoke from my heart: "Please forgive me for not honoring you as I should." My words were raw and sincere—a collective plea for the mistreatment of women throughout history to be acknowledged. This act of deep surrender sparked an internal shift, releasing guilt, shame, and the burden of unspoken regrets.

A facilitator approached gently, advising me to lower my voice. The environment was sacred and intended for healing, and loudness could disrupt the delicate atmosphere essential for the ceremony's full flourishing. While his voice conveyed kindness, a slight wave of embarrassment surged through me. So immersed in my emotional landscape, I had lost sight of the larger surroundings, allowing my feelings to spill over inappropriately. I recognized the balance required in the ceremony, honoring both the sanctity of the space and the people around me.

The facilitator's reminder did not hinder me; instead, it anchored me in the moment. I took a deep breath, refocused my thoughts, and processed the intense emotions that surfaced. The forgiveness I sought emerged as essential, allowing me to reconcile with my past decisions and enabling me to advance with a renewed sense of lightness. Within the depths of the ceremony, I became aware of the profound healing energy emanating not just from the medicine but also through insight and atonement. I recognized that this moment marked a crucial milestone in my personal growth, one that would stay with me well beyond the ceremony's end.

Mother Ayahuasca's message echoed through the quiet recesses of my being: she had summoned me to this sanctuary two years ago for a distinct purpose. At that moment, I was oblivious to the weight of her intentions. She revealed that my previous experience had been a preparation designed to cultivate a sacred environment, primed for the extraordinary event that had just unfolded. The importance of that initial journey crystallized; it was a time for spiritual growth, enhancing my connection to the divine energies surrounding me.

I returned—fully cognizant and equipped—because my purpose was to safeguard the noble soul present and the goddesses who accompanied him, creating a safe space for the celestial forces that would guide this ceremony. The gravity of her message settled deep within my heart, serving as a reminder that the path ahead demanded I embrace a mantle of vigilance, protection, and sacred duty, a realization that had only just begun to take root within me.

Lying on my mat, I began to contemplate the immense experience I had just traversed. Vivid visions and sounds filled my mind as I sought clarity on the significant events that had transpired. Each fleeting moment resonated with profound meaning, even as I felt I was grasping at ephemeral truths. The participants' faces hovered in my thoughts, their expressions reflecting awe and trepidation as if they had all glimpsed something beyond ordinary perception. I understood we were gathered for a reason, each carrying unique burdens and lessons waiting to be uncovered. In this sacred space, we had shared those weights, even if only briefly, connecting on a level that surpassed words and physical boundaries.

Sleep eluded me despite my exhaustion. The ceremony's potent energy and the weight of revelations reverberated through my being. As I closed my eyes, the images and sensations resurfaced with heightened intensity. The medicine had opened a gateway I couldn't shut, leaving me suspended in a liminal space—caught between wakefulness and slumber. The weight of both personal and universal revelations made resting impossible. My thoughts spiraled endlessly, striving to unpack the profound meanings embedded within the experience.

I felt like a vessel brimming with ancient insights and new realizations, yet a sense of uncertainty about containing it all lingered. I was not merely stranded with my thoughts but intricately connected to something immensely greater—an energy that was both comforting and overwhelming. The weight of this connection pressed heavily within me, making sleep even more unattainable. Yet, I recognized that this was part of the process, part of the journey I had embraced. The healing, understanding, and transformation were neither solely physical nor limited to one aspect of my being; they engaged my mind, emotions, and soul, requiring time for full integration. I lay there, awake in the tranquil aftermath, pondering the depths of what had been set in motion.

As the first light of dawn pierced the dense jungle canopy, tranquility enveloped me. The air was fresh and revitalizing, scented with the earthy essence of nature stirring to life. Before me stood the lady shaman, holding a bowl filled with water infused with vibrant petals that seemed to capture the very spirit of the morning. The cold water mix saturated the air with soothing, aromatic fragrances. As the water cascaded over me, it felt as if the spirit of the jungle was purging my soul, washing away the traces of the tumultuous night behind me.

With each cool droplet that glided down my skin, the burdens of the prior night gradually faded, making way for profound serenity. Each gentle kiss of the petals felt like a comforting embrace—both soothing and revitalizing. The holy water not only cleansed my body but also nurtured my spirit, dissipating tension, uncertainty, and the weight of previous visions. I felt as though I was enveloped in an ancient, warm embrace that transcended both time and space.

The vivid memories and insights from the ceremony would not vanish; they lingered in the background, pulsating with life, their importance vividly present within me. The floral bath instilled tranquility in my body, yet my spirit remained tethered to the experiences of the previous night. The truths that were revealed to me felt engraved in my very core, palpable symbols that could not be ignored. The depths of what transpired left an indelible mark—one that would echo for a long time.

After the curandera completed the purification ritual, I stood in silence, absorbing the peaceful energy surrounding me. The jungle awakened with vibrant sounds, mirroring the stillness settling within me. Though the visions of the previous evening had not faded, clarity began to emerge. The bath's gentle healing power created space for me to process, assimilate, and gradually comprehend what I had witnessed. This moment marked the beginning of a new chapter, a time to reflect on the transformative journey I had undertaken while preparing for the forthcoming work of healing and understanding.

As sunlight filtered through the lush Amazon canopy, casting intricate patterns on the ground, I found myself seated on the wooden steps of the retreat's communal area. This serene haven, nestled among the jungle, provided a perfect sanctuary for contemplation and rest, its tranquility enhancing my reflective state. In this calming environment, where I sat alongside my Indian brother and fellow participants, our conversation flowed effortlessly, as though we shared a deep-rooted bond. Yet, beneath this calm façade, a question I had long carried clamored for attention.

I could no longer restrain the question that had haunted me since the ceremony. It stirred doubts and curiosity within me, demanding resolution. Turning to my Indian brother, I gazed into his eyes, seeking answers. "Is what Mother Ayahuasca told me about you true?" I asked, my voice steady but burdened with uncertainty. His gaze remained unwavering, and his expression was calm. Without delay, he nodded. "It is true," he affirmed, his voice composed and filled with quiet assurance.

Relief surged through me upon his acknowledgment, dissipating the lingering doubts that had clouded my mind. However, this sense of relief quickly morphed into a mix of confusion and frustration. If it was true, why had he remained silent when I shared my profound insights with the group? A wave of frustration rose within me as I sought clarity. "Then why didn't you speak up when I shared my experience with everyone?" I asked, recalling the doubtful and often dismissive expressions I received from the group in response to my revelations as if they thought I had lost a few marbles. His simple yet profound reply struck me deeply.

"They are not ready, brother," he stated quietly, imbued with wisdom beyond mere words. His response conveyed no judgment or blame; instead, it resonated with an understanding that intertwined deeply with my own. I grasped that not everyone was prepared to accept such truths; not everyone could receive the message as intended. The essence of truth could not be forced upon those unprepared to embrace it. His words settled in my consciousness, reminding me that some lessons must unfold at their own pace. The path toward awakening was uniquely personal; each of us had our journey to traverse.

His response left me contemplating, with the answer both enlightening and perplexing. "But how could I possibly know these things?" I exclaimed, desperation and disbelief woven into my inquiry. I was grasping for a thread of clarity, a tangible explanation for the strange connection I increasingly felt toward forces beyond comprehension. His gaze softened, and his calm demeanor grounded me amid my inner tempest. With a gentle smile, he replied, "You know because you are Rudhra." His words reverberated deep within me despite my inability to fully grasp their meaning at that moment.

The name "Rudhra" was unfamiliar, leading me to seek any references or understanding within my knowledge base. It felt ancient and powerful, yet utterly foreign. I furrowed my brow in searching thoughts, but nothing clicked. "Who is Rudhra?" I inquired, my curiosity ignited as if trying to unravel a profound mystery. His smile widened as if anticipating this very question. Meeting my gaze, his eyes sparkled with knowledge as he responded, "Rudhra is an avatar of Shiva."

His response struck me like a sudden illumination; for a moment, I struggled to voice my thoughts. The idea of a connection to Shiva, a deity I had only encountered in fragments, was breathtakingly surreal. As the God of destruction and transformation within Hindu lore, Shiva occupied a crucial space in the cycles of creation, preservation, and dissolution in the universe. He was more than a mere figure; he represented the very paradox of existence, embodying creation and destruction, detachment and compassion, both asceticism and profound love.

Rudhra, the name my brother had spoken, was one of the many forms of Shiva. In Hindu tradition, Rudhra is often considered the fierce, untamed aspect of Shiva—an incarnation of the Divine that represents the raw, destructive power necessary for the regeneration of the world. Rudra's name itself is associated with "roar" or "howl," symbolizing the primal force of the universe that sweeps away the old to make room for the new. He is the embodiment of both compassion and wrath, a deity who frees souls from their attachments and worldly illusions, creating the space for spiritual awakening. His role is not merely one of destruction but of transformation—a force that clears away the clutter of the ego and the false self to reveal the truth that lies beneath.

Stunned by his explanation, I sat in silence, trying to process the enormity of his words. Could it be possible that I was somehow linked to this powerful, transcendent force? I stared at my brother, trying to reconcile the image of Rudhra with the person I thought I was. "How do you know this?" I finally managed to ask, my voice trembling with the weight of the question. He met my gaze with steady confidence, his answer simple yet profound: "I was told." His words hung in the air, and I could feel the depth of his conviction. "I asked twice to be sure," he continued, "and both times, the answer was the same." There was no hesitation in his voice, no doubt. At that moment, I understood that his certainty came not from speculation but from a profound, intuitive knowing —a knowing that had been passed to him through his journey and experiences. The answer felt like a key to a door that had been locked for lifetimes, and I had just glimpsed the way forward.

The resonance of his truth sank deeply into my being, reverberating through my essence. His profound statement unearthed an awareness within me—a dormant truth longing to be acknowledged. The building in front of us began to shift, with familiar surroundings becoming charged with an energy that felt ancient. The retreat's communal space, once a haven of reflection, pulsated with an intangible current infused with a revelation waiting to be discovered.

The wooden steps beneath us, once solid and stable, now vibrated with a resonance I couldn't fully fathom. Each plank felt like a vessel of ancient wisdom, echoing a profound truth that transcended time. The ambiance blurred as my attention fell away from the external, sinking into the depths of this new awareness. I felt wrapped in a reality that reached far beyond the physical, tethered to something vast and interconnected.

My brother's steady confidence anchored me in the midst of a storm of emotions. With every word he shared, he planted a seed of understanding deep within my heart. Though slight in its initial fragility, this seed contained the potential for something expansive. It was a truth I could not fully comprehend; however, I sensed its growth would reshape my being. His quiet conviction invited me to step onto a path both unknown and remarkably familiar. There was no urgency, no pressure—only the serene assurance that I was embarking on a journey meant for my soul, with answers waiting to align as I readied myself to embrace them.

A stir within me ignited a change in my perspective, as though the veil separating the known from the unknown had slightly lifted. This was more than a transient moment; it heralded the beginning of a profound awakening, one that would blossom gradually, akin to a flower unfurling or a new chapter unfolding in an ever-evolving narrative. I realized that the journey ahead would not yield immediate answers but would promise continuous revelations, with each step offering insights into both myself and the world around me. With this understanding, I recognized that I was already traversing the path I had sought, even if the complete picture remained elusive.

Chapter Seven

Lessons in Humility

The weight of my previous ceremonies remained in my thoughts; the vivid visions and emotional releases echoed within me. I approached the third ceremony with cautious reverence. The anticipation that once filled me with exuberance was now imbued with a deeper energy—one of respect and thoughtful deliberation. I had learned to navigate the presence of such formidable forces with care, aware that Mother Ayahuasca unveils truths in her own time and manner. This time, I opted for just one cup, aiming to maintain a degree of lightness regarding the situation ahead. I didn't want to dive too quickly into the unknown, yet I understood the importance of being ready for whatever might occur.

The night commenced with profound stillness. The hushed whispers of my brothers and sisters faded into obscurity. I hoped this ceremony would feel lighter; perhaps it would be gentler and softer than the previous one. The familiar sounds of the jungle —the rustling foliage and distant calls—formed a tranquil backdrop. As the shaman approached me, I felt a noticeable change in the atmosphere. His presence commanded attention without uttering a word. He began to sing a powerful icaro, its melody rich with ancient wisdom. As the song grew in intensity, I found myself irresistibly drawn to its rhythm. The shaman's voice echoed within me, awakening a deep, instinctual response.

To my surprise, the shaman offered me a bottle of water. This unexpected gesture left me feeling unsettled. Why was he offering water? I didn't remember it being an integral part of the ceremony. I hesitated, unsure of its meaning. His gentle encouragement urged me forward, and I took a cautious sip. The refreshing liquid flowed down my throat, bringing a brief but welcome sensation of tranquility. He prompted me for another sip, which I accepted, though uncertainty still lingered. A persistent thought crept in—something essential was on the verge of changing, though I couldn't quite grasp the reason.

As the second sip coursed through me, a wave of vitality surged through me, more intense and immediate than anything I had ever experienced. My senses heightened, and an overwhelming pressure built within me. Before I fully comprehended what was happening, I found myself bent over the bucket, the force of my expulsion consuming me. This moment eclipsed any prior release; it felt as though I were unearthing something deeply entrenched within my core.

The following day, fueled by both curiosity and amazement, I approached the facilitators to inquire whether it was typical for the shaman to share his water with the participants. To my amazement, they exchanged incredulous looks and shook their heads. This unexpected act intensified the enigma of the previous night. Why did the shaman ask me to take those sips of water? What deeper meaning did this gesture carry? These questions swirled in my mind, complicating the events of the evening. I realized that this seemingly routine moment was infused with significance—potentially a subtle act of faith or an invitation to embrace a transformation I had yet to fully grasp.

When I looked into the bucket, there were no clear traces of what had been purged—no remnants or physical signs of the darkness I had just expelled. Instead, resting at the bottom appeared to be a motionless creature resembling a beetle, about two to three inches long. Its presence seemed symbolic, suggesting that a deeper transformation had taken place. The beetle felt like a manifestation of the energies I had released—fears, traumas, and ancestral baggage—things long buried within me. The absence of any true physical substance in the bucket was a reminder that the purge had been a profound spiritual release. The beetle's stillness spoke of quiet acceptance. Its motionless form felt like a message: what had once been dark, turbulent, and heavy had been integrated into something more peaceful. Although its exact significance remained unclear, I sensed that it was a messenger of change, marking the shedding of old layers.

As I began to rise from my position, preparing to return to my mat, Mother Ayahuasca's voice pierced through the stillness of my mind, halting me. It wasn't merely a whisper; it felt like a directive—one impossible to disregard. She demanded that I remain in a submissive posture, emphasizing the importance of her teachings. Her tone bore no harshness but held a sharp clarity. It was not the kind of sharpness that aimed to wound but one that sought to awaken, peeling away layers of illusion and self-deception. In her presence, the pretense was cast aside; only truth remained, regardless of its discomfort. As I stayed there, still and attentive, I felt a profound reverence for her words, knowing they emanated from deep wisdom and love.

Her voice wrapped around me like an embrace, delivering a message that pierced the core of my identity. She spoke with precision, highlighting that my confidence—viewed by me as strength—could sometimes be misinterpreted by others, particularly men, as arrogance. In my interactions, I believed my confidence reflected genuine self-belief. However, through her guidance, I began to see that confidence could be perceived negatively if unaccompanied by humility and self-awareness. This realization struck me profoundly, shedding light on how others might receive my energy. Although my intentions were rooted in authenticity, intentions alone couldn't capture the scope of my impact on those around me.

She continued, shifting her focus to how I related to women—a topic that resonated deeply within me. Despite my sincere efforts to treat others with kindness and respect, she revealed that my demeanor could sometimes appear intimidating or even threatening. This realization emerged from a moment of acute awareness—my gestures, tone, and unheeded energy might have fostered discomfort or fear in women. My longing to connect and express my feelings frequently overshadowed more subtle ways to create a safe and welcoming space for others. This insight redefined my understanding; good intentions alone fell short;

they needed to align with how others perceived my energy.

Her message was straightforward yet profound: it's not merely our intentions that count but also how others experience our energy. This lesson in humility emphasized that our presence in the world —deliberate or not—holds more profound implications. I started to recognize that personal growth involves refining my intentions and adjusting my energy and behavior to encourage openness and understanding from others. This realization cultivated empathy, allowing me to view the world through others' perspectives. I understood that this experience would shape my future relationships, fostering deeper connections and harmony.

Mother Ayahuasca guided me back to a defining moment in my past, drawing me into a memory I had long tried to forget. I was seventeen, standing on the threshold of adulthood, with my emotions intense and raw. As I relived my first experience of love, I felt the thrill, vulnerability, and joy that accompanied those early feelings. However, beneath the excitement lay something dark—a painful truth that lingered unresolved. I saw myself at that time, caught up in the rush of desire and youthful impulsiveness, unable to see the harm I was causing. In my pursuit of love, I betrayed a friend—someone who had stood by my side throughout my youth. The weight of the betrayal struck me like a sharp blow, with guilt twisting deep within my chest.

The memory resurfaced with a wave of remorse, a shadow that had silently followed me for years. I became the lover of the woman my friend cherished, ignoring the pain I was inflicting on him in my selfish pursuit. My desire for her love, so strong and consuming, blinded me to the consequences of my actions, and I couldn't fathom the damage I had inflicted on the person who had been closest to me.

I chose love over loyalty and convinced myself it was worth it, but now the reality of that betrayal hits me with full force. I could see the pain in his eyes again—the deep sense of betrayal he must have felt when he realized I had put my desires before his friendship. The weight of that moment, the unspoken hurt, flooded over me anew. The guilt came rushing back, unrelenting and fresh, as though time had never passed.

Mother Ayahuasca's presence was both tender and resolute, offering me lessons through that painful episode. She nudged me to confront the consequences of my actions, to acknowledge the hurt I had inflicted and the suffering that arose from my choices. No chastisement accompanied her voice; she afforded me the space to deeply feel my regret, allowing it to move through me. This experience proved challenging but essential. I had to face the version of myself who made that choice —unable to evade the burden of my decisions. The guilt swelled within me, highlighting that the moment transcended remorse; it was about growth, recognizing our actions' ramifications, and seeking redemption—even if that redemption was solely internal.

With a deep breath, I whispered an apology, understanding my words would never reach the one I wronged. It was not about seeking forgiveness from him; it was about granting forgiveness to myself for past mistakes and letting go of the guilt that had taunted me for years. As I uttered the apology, I felt a weight lift from my chest—a relief born from acknowledging the past and pursuing healing. Even as the burden faded, the truth of my past actions remained—a reminder of the complexity woven into our choices. It was a humbling lesson that emphasized the importance of integrity, compassion, and the understanding that our actions ripple across time, affecting lives in ways we may never fully grasp.

As the night unfolded, I remained motionless on my mat, immersed in a deep exploration of my thoughts. Vivid memories played in my mind—each moment revealing a clearer perspective. I witnessed the narrative of my life, marked by flashes of brilliance and shadowy depths. I reflected on instances where I had caused pain—not only to others but also to myself. The familiar burdens of guilt and regret intensified in my heart, making each decision feel profoundly impactful. In those moments, I felt utterly empty, as if there were nothing left of "me," "mine," or "I." It was as if the very essence of self had dissolved, leaving behind only awareness. I understood that every choice carries weight, shaping the individual I have become.

Through introspection, I uncovered profound patterns—insecurities, anxieties, and longings that shaped my choices. Often propelled by a craving for affirmation or a dread of rejection, I acted without thinking of the consequences. These hidden drives led me down paths that initially seemed to offer comfort or fulfillment but ultimately resulted in anguish. As I revisited these experiences, I felt deep regret for those I had hurt, even as time allowed their wounds to mend. It was not just the damage inflicted that troubled me but also the ways in which I compromised my principles, deceived by false notions of control and certainty. The awareness that my lack of self-reflection governed my decisions struck me as a subtle yet profound awakening.

As the night progressed, the repercussions of my errors became starkly apparent. It transcended the visible fallout of damaged relationships and lost chances; it penetrated my core. The past could not be changed, but I understood that it need not govern my future. The road ahead demanded that I unite the disjointed fragments of my being, repair the harm I had caused others, and cultivate inner forgiveness. Only by doing so could I move forward, releasing the burden of remorse and evolving into a more self-aware individual.

As the ceremony came to a close, a serene stillness settled over the night, and my thoughts began to slow. The flood of realizations merged into a calm reflection. My body loosened as the strain from hours of introspection faded away. Sleep, which had long been elusive, now extended a warm invitation. However, as I surrendered to rest, the lessons I learned stayed intricately embedded within me. A quiet determination took shape—recognizing that personal growth is gradual, requiring patience, humility, and the courage to face uncomfortable realities.

The next morning, I immersed myself in the floral bath that felt remarkably revitalizing. The water, infused with colorful petals, cascaded over my skin, providing a cleansing and nourishing experience that transcended mere hygiene. It seemed to embody the very essence of the jungle, offering more than just a rinse. Each droplet cleared away not only the remnants of the ceremony but also the burdens that weighed on my soul. The soft petals against my skin reminded me of nature's gentle presence, encouraging me to release what no longer served my growth. This ordinary ritual evolved into a significant act of renewal, prompting reflection and a fresh start.

As I felt the last droplets fall away from my skin, I acknowledged the preciousness of this serene morning. It wasn't the anticipated flashes of insight that emerged but rather a profound connection to the lessons I had previously internalized. The simplicity of this ritual enabled me to embrace those teachings fully, anchoring me firmly in the present. I felt lighter and more centered, as if a transformation had taken place—not in my surroundings but within myself. The weight of my past felt less burdensome; while I recognized the long journey ahead, I sensed a greater readiness to navigate it with grace and understanding.

Although this ceremony did not produce the vivid visions I had experienced previously, the energy of the morning felt equally potent yet different. It lacked the exhilarating bursts of revelation or the overwhelming intensity of the medicine. Instead, it revealed a steady, serene clarity. Mother Ayahuasca's influence remained palpable, her insights intricately woven into the fabric of the experience. I surrendered to the gentle ebb of the bath, absorbing her wisdom—a profound, persistent current that imparted the significance of gentleness and empathy, both toward others and myself.

I felt a strong desire to act with mindfulness, recognizing the ripple effect of my words and choices. An emphasis on empathy emerged, nudging me to prevent my ego from clouding my interactions and to engage with others compassionately. Mother Ayahuasca communicated that genuine growth arises not from grand gestures but from the small, consistent choices we make each day. These seemingly minor actions and moments of compassion will chart my path in ways I have yet to explore.

Chapter Eight

The Warrior's Gift

As the final evening of the second retreat approached, I was filled with a profound sense of respect for the upcoming ceremony. This event emanated a sense of holiness; an unvoiced energy filled the maloca. I drank a single cup of Ayahuasca, drawing on the wisdom gained from previous ceremonies. I was ready to absorb the lessons that Mother Ayahuasca had in store for me. A tangible sense of eagerness hung in the air, suggesting that the maloca was preparing for a momentous experience. A storm had been brewing for hours, with dark clouds gathering ominously on the horizon. As the shamans began their opening icaros, the tempest erupted. The skies unleashed a downpour upon the maloca, creating a deafening and urgent soundscape. It felt as if nature itself had joined our sacred gathering, heightening the energy with every thunderous clap. The charged atmosphere reflected the imminent intensity of the ceremony.

What had started as a tropical shower quickly escalated into torrential rain, matching the fervor of the ceremony. The wind howled, whipping through the trees and bending their branches in violent arcs as if the jungle itself were responding to the energetic shifts within. The maloca seemed alive, swaying in rhythm with the storm's fury as though it were a sentient being bracing against the forces outside. The rain lashed against the wooden walls, its roar drowning out all but the sounds of nature's tumultuous power. Lightning ripped through the sky in sudden bursts, illuminating the surroundings with blinding brilliance while the ground trembled beneath the weight of the storm's crescendo. The growing fury of the tempest mirrored the surging energy within the maloca, amplifying the intensity of the ceremony in a profound, almost mystical way. The elements outside were intricately tied to the unseen forces at play within our sacred space.

As the storm amplified, the thunder became deafening, its roar so powerful that it seemed to shake the very air we breathed. The sound reverberated through the maloca, harmonizing with the deep, resonant chants of the shamans, creating an otherworldly synergy between the elements and the sacred rites. The energy in the room intensified as if the storm and the ceremony were part of the same divine performance. The torrential rain, now a deafening symphony, echoed like the voice of the universe itself, as if nature were joining in our spiritual unfolding. Despite the overwhelming noise, the shamans' icaros pierced through, their sacred melodies carrying the essence of the ceremony into the heart of the storm. The relentless downpour seemed to embody the powerful purification occurring within each of us as we were swept into the depths of our transformation, guided by the storm and the wisdom of the medicine.

Men and women occupied separate spaces, adhering to tradition, with each group claiming its respective side of the maloca. This separation felt more pronounced than before, as if the storm visually echoed the internal divisions with which we often wrestle. Yet, there was a sense of unity as the storm and the ceremony forged a connection that urged us toward deeper understanding. The storm's ceaseless energy compelled us to remain present, demanding our attention to the turmoil within and around us, free from distraction. It was a call to embrace the chaos, surrender to the flow of the universe, and trust that clarity would emerge from the tumult.

As the storm unleashed its fury outside, the lamentations of the women filled the maloca, intertwining with nature's wrath. Their anguish transformed the space into a vortex of emotion, creating an atmosphere thick with suffering that echoed the storm beyond. Each cry unleashed deep-seated pain, unfiltered and primeval. The energy within the maloca surged, crackling with the intensity of their emotional releases. In this tumult, Mother Ayahuasca's steadfast presence cut through the disorder, her calm reaching me amid the overwhelming noise.

She awakened a powerful sense of my inner strength, calling forth the energy of my warrior spirit. In that sacred moment, Mother Ayahuasca revealed something profound: a woman participating in the ceremony embodied the energy of what I had long believed was my missing half. Her words sparked a surge of joy and purpose within me. I realized that this connection went beyond physical attraction; it was a deep spiritual bond, an alignment of energies meant to unite. Mother Ayahuasca assured me that while this woman needed time for her growth, our paths would ultimately intersect at the right moment. I accepted this message with conviction, believing it held a definitive truth about this remarkable young woman.

As I reflected over time, I understood that Mother Ayahuasca had not been referring to a specific individual. What I had initially taken as a message about a particular woman revealed a much deeper truth about energy itself. I came to realize that she was not speaking of a person but of Shakti, the Divine Feminine force. My limited knowledge at that time led me to misinterpret her message. In hindsight, it was clear that Mother Ayahuasca was guiding me to awaken the Shakti energy both within myself and in the world around me—an energy that transcends form and connects everything.

This realization unfolded gradually. I began to comprehend that Shakti exists within all of us, perpetually flowing and transforming, not confined to a singular identity. The woman I perceived as my "missing half" reflected this expansive, universal energy, manifesting as the Divine Feminine I had yet to fully acknowledge. Mother Ayahuasca's words were a call to awaken to this energy, to honor and integrate the sacred feminine in all its manifestations—beyond any singular individual—embodying an energy central to the universe's balance. This lesson represented spiritual growth and awareness that invited me to transcend narrow understandings and embrace a broader vision of connection and wholeness.

Filled with gratitude, I inquired how I could repay Mother Ayahuasca for her guidance. Her wisdom had navigated me through inner chaos and clarified my path beyond my ability to articulate. She offered clear and meaningful advice: "Focus only on yourself and the goddesses; disregard all else," she asserted. Her message felt weighty, not as a directive but as a gentle nudge toward centering my energy on what mattered most. Then, her tone softened yet remained resolute. "The goddesses are in pain, and they are very dear to me." Her words radiated compassion, urging me to honor the feminine energy that she cherished. This was a reminder that by prioritizing my growth, I could simultaneously honor the Divine Feminine, contributing to the greater healing unfolding around me.

With resolute intent, I offered my assistance, feeling awakened to a profound responsibility. The ceremony's weight, the storm's fury, and the raw emotions swirling around me sparked a desire to alleviate the suffering I witnessed. I yearned to be of service, to offer part of myself in return for the immense healing I had received. Without hesitation, I asked, "Mother, may I help?" Her presence, ever tranquil and wise, paused for a moment, contemplating my offer. A stillness enveloped the room before she replied.

She inquired, "What do you have in mind?" I responded promptly, explaining my thoughts. "You once transferred the burdens of others to me," I reminded her, referencing a time when she had guided me in taking on the suffering of my former military crew members. "Could I do the same now to help with the goddesses' suffering?" I asked, my voice imbued with sincerity. I believed this path was mine to walk—a way to contribute to the collective healing enveloping the maloca. The idea of absorbing the anguish of others felt like a natural extension of the work I was meant to do.

This time, Mother Ayahuasca responded differently. She kindly guided me, presenting a new perspective on the task I had in mind. "This time, it must be approached differently," she stated, her voice infused with an unexpected depth of wisdom. Her answer was neither dismissive nor harsh but firm, implying that my suggestion, while well-meaning, was not suitable for this moment. A pause followed, and I felt her energy shift, guiding me toward a deeper understanding of how to help—one that transcended merely absorbing pain and embraced a more holistic view of healing.

I sensed that something more profound lay within this task beyond what I had initially envisioned. Mother Ayahuasca taught me that healing does not revolve around taking on others' suffering; instead, it requires comprehending the essence of that suffering and finding a meaningful way to assist in harmonizing with my growth and the growth of those I aim to support. This new approach urged me to expand beyond previous methods, tapping into a deeper wisdom that focused on empowerment for both myself and others rather than self-sacrifice.

She instructed me to kneel, thrusting my chest forward as an open target for the goddesses to project their pain, fears, and darkest nightmares onto me. Following her guidance, I positioned myself as she directed, bracing for the forthcoming surge of energy. A sudden and powerful force erupted toward me. I saw and felt fiery, energetic projectiles aimed directly at my heart, each wave more intense than the last. This energy was not merely a sensation; it embodied a force carrying the weight of the goddesses' anguish. Each impact felt as if an indescribable wave of emotion pierced through me, demanding acknowledgment.

A force of divine destruction and transformation has been fully unleashed within me. This power surged through me, a force so fierce and uncontainable that it seemed as if the entire cosmos echoed with the primal roar of its awakening. The cacophony grew deafening as if the very world were responding to the magnitude of the suffering I was embracing. The fury of the storm and the energy coursing through me merged, creating a powerful resonance that filled every crevice of the space, as though the universe had synchronized with the pain and healing occurring within and around me.

The agony was unbearable, unlike any suffering I had previously encountered. I felt my heart being dismantled piece by piece by their collective burden. I sensed the depth of their trauma—years, perhaps lifetimes, of sorrow that had sought refuge within. My very being became a vessel for their pain, and each surge felt more torturous than the last. My chest constricted, and each breath felt lodged in my throat as I absorbed their shared anguish.

Outside, the storm mirrored the growing turbulence within me. Thunder escalated, its deep, resonant roar shaking the very ground beneath the maloca and syncing with the intensifying energy coursing through my body. The rain pounded relentlessly against the roof as though nature itself were unleashing its fury. The wind howled, rattling the wooden walls as the storm reached its peak—a violent crescendo that reverberated through every fiber of my being.

I transformed into a container for their anguish, carrying a weight far too burdensome for a single soul. Through this sacred exchange of vulnerability, I recognized that I was not merely absorbing their suffering; I was enabling its release. Each surge of grief I experienced faded little by little, easing the load for the goddesses who had endured it for ages. With each release, I felt a profound transformation—a metamorphosis where sorrow evolved into something more manageable, no longer just distress but a pathway toward healing.

I endured the agony, grasping every bit of my dwindling strength as energy coursed through me uncontrollably. It felt like an arduous battle, each second dragging me further into despair, yet I remained steadfast, recognizing that this ordeal was essential for their healing. Eventually, after what seemed like an endless stretch of time, the agony began to fade. Leaning forward, an overpowering urge compelled me to expel. I summoned all my strength, my body quaking as darkness erupted from within, pouring into the bucket positioned in front of me. This release unleashed a torrent of grotesque, distorted visions—shadows and shapes that violently rushed through my mind. The expulsion felt boundless; every fiber of my being expelled the accumulated grief, fears, and burdens of countless lifetimes.

As the darkness receded, the storm outside, which had mirrored my inner turmoil, gradually calmed. The thunder shifted to a faint whisper, and the relentless rain transformed into a soft cadence. The environment outside released a collective sigh, shedding the storm's heavy burden. Inside the maloca, the anguished cries of the goddesses that had once resonated in the space faded into soothing quiet. The chaos evolved into serene tranquility, enshrouding the room. The energy that had once surged wildly settled into a gentle flow, and the atmosphere lightened, harmonizing with a comforting undertone of healing. The once-tormented goddesses now found tranquility, their souls embraced by the profound stillness surrounding us.

As the final remnants of darkness departed from me, I felt the familiar presence of Mother Ayahuasca once more. Her energy wrapped around me like a warm embrace—gentle yet potent, soothing like a balm after a storm. Her voice, serene and wise, echoed in my mind with a soft resonance. "I brought you here for this purpose," she said, her tone tender yet profound. "Because you volunteered, I have a gift for you." Her words settled within my heart, stirring deep gratitude and astonishment. "You don't need to do anything," she continued. "Just be patient."

I lingered in the surrounding silence, a quiet reverence consuming me. There was no rush, no urgency for action. Healing had emerged, and now I could rest, trusting in the unfolding of everything as it was meant to be. I felt a calmness settling in, and within that serenity, a quiet joy blossomed inside me. I was liberated from the weight of prior burdens; I had found freedom.

Her promise felt both reassuring and enigmatic. She sought nothing but my trust, and with that simple request, assurance washed over me. I sensed no urgency to grasp every detail immediately; all I needed was faith. Mother Ayahuasca reflected on the previous ceremony, articulating that she had prepared me by emptying my ego and cleansing anything that could obstruct my forthcoming work. This journey was not about confrontation but love, carrying the strength of my affection for my daughter and the high-ranking goddess who enabled me to endure this spiritual endeavor. I grasped the sacredness of the ceremony, the significance of each step taken, and the essential role love played in my process. Every experience and challenge has been pivotal in guiding me to this moment of clarity.

The ceremony's conclusion, while dreamlike, carried a profound sense of fulfillment. A serene calm descended as if the cosmos had perfectly synchronized. The jungle beyond had hushed, its sounds mirroring the inner peace that enveloped me. Although I could not sleep, I felt no restlessness. I lay in quiet acknowledgment of having realized my purpose in that sacred space. The teachings, energies, and divine presence I encountered remained within me, a lasting echo of the love and transformation I had undergone. This was not just a fleeting experience but a significant evolution nestled within my being.

As dawn broke, the air stirred with vibrant life. The final floral bath served as a tender offering of sacred water and herbs akin to a divine anointing. As the cool water embraced me, it felt like a soothing shroud, solidifying the profound change I had experienced. Each droplet embodied the essence of the jungle, the ancient wisdom of the ceremony, and the love of Mother Ayahuasca. This concluding act marked a culmination, cleansing not only my physical being but also my very soul. The aromas of the flowers and herbs filled me with profound gratitude and tranquility, creating a perfect closure to my second retreat. I emerged complete, rejuvenated, and deeply attuned to the divine energy that had guided me throughout.

Chapter Nine

The Warrior's Path

After my second retreat at Nimea Kaya Sanctuary, I found myself engulfed in profound self-reflection as the complex layers of my experience gradually unraveled, each revealing a deeper, undeniable truth underlying everything I had encountered. The ceremonies were not isolated experiences; rather, they formed an intricate continuum woven seamlessly into a rich tapestry of meaning and discovery. This spectrum of experiences sharply contrasted with the reflections shared by my fellow participants.

During our group discussions, I immersed myself in the compelling stories shared by others about their personal experiences. Many narrated extraordinary moments that varied significantly from one ceremony to another, including fleeting visions of otherworldly beings, cryptic insights from Mother Ayahuasca, and fragmented recollections of occurrences that felt disconnected from their present realities. Their narratives fascinated me, yet they often lacked the continuous thread that characterized my path. Each participant navigated a distinct tapestry of revelations, but none appeared to follow a unified, coherent journey.

My experiences felt more like chapters in an unfolding narrative than fragmented episodes. This story had begun long before my arrival at the sanctuary and would likely continue long after my departure. I felt as though I were being led through an endless series of gateways, each opening to a realm that expanded my understanding of both myself and the universe. With each ceremony, a layer of pretense was peeled away, exposing a fundamental truth that lay concealed beneath.

Some might argue that I was hallucinating, that my experiences were constructs of my mind—products of the brew or my subconscious. What could be more commonplace than the mind-generating images and stories in altered states? Yet, the continuity of these experiences went beyond the logic of ordinary hallucination. Each revelation was not an isolated event but was intrinsically linked to the one before, as if an invisible thread were weaving through the fabric of my awareness, leading me toward greater understanding. It wasn't random; it had a purpose, like a path unfolding with deliberate intent.

Even more remarkable was the fact that this continuity persisted even after a lengthy pause between ceremonies. The first time I encountered Mother Ayahuasca was two years prior, but when I returned, the journey resumed exactly where it had left off. How could this happen? After all, my life had been consumed by day-to-day realities—how could my mind retain such intricate threads of awareness over such a long period? How could memories, insights, and lessons from previous ceremonies resurface so clearly, as though no time had passed? The seamless progression of my journey, how it picked up right where it had stopped, could not be explained away by ordinary mental processes.

It became apparent that these experiences were not just my mind creating hallucinations but something much deeper. What I was engaging with was not merely internal; it extended beyond the limits of my perception, revealing knowledge, wisdom, and realms of existence that existed outside my mind's fabrication. Each moment of this journey built upon the last, contributing to a greater narrative—a story not dictated by me but by an external truth that was patiently waiting to be revealed. This continuity, along with the increasing depth of what was being unveiled, pointed toward something much grander than my own experience—an interconnectedness that defied explanation and suggested a higher order governing all existence.

Descending this slope proved to be quite demanding. Each doorway presented obstacles and revelations that compelled me to confront deeply buried fears, uncertainties, and existential questions. Yet, there was a rhythm to it all, a sense that each step was part of a purposeful journey—a cosmic curriculum tailored uniquely for me. I was not merely participating in ceremonies; I was engaged in a conversation with something far greater—an energy with the intent of unveiling the essence of my true identity.

This sense of continuity infused my journey with a profound purpose, as if I was on a sacred journey requiring not just understanding but the embodiment of the truths that were being revealed.

With each ceremony, the veil dividing the ordinary from the Divine grew thinner, leading me to recognize that the answers I sought lay not outside but within, waiting to be unearthed from the depths of my being.

My experiences were purposeful, directed by an invisible energy with a clear objective: to help me uncover something profound. Each encounter with Mother Ayahuasca centered around a fundamental truth. These insights were not mere fleeting glimpses but pieces of a larger puzzle. As I began to assemble them, a profound understanding surfaced: I was a guardian of timeless knowledge and eternal truths.

This realization transcended the realm of comforting notions and metaphors; it felt as though the very essence of my being was undergoing a rediscovery. These ceremonies represented more than spiritual experiences; they were acts of remembrance, peeling away the layers of my constructed identity to reveal something pure, instinctive, and everlasting. With every insight, I was reconnecting with a dimension of myself that had always existed and was now revealed beneath years of doubt, distractions, and social programming.

The deeper I probed my experiences, the clearer it became that this journey was not about assuming a role or fulfilling a task. It was about embodying a truth that had always dwelled within me, suggesting that I was being meticulously prepared for something far more significant than my current understanding—an experience that transcended my limitations and connected me to the collective consciousness permeating the universe.

The visions were vibrant and visceral but carried layers of symbolism that transcended their immediate images. They served as whispers of a destiny that was both personal and collective, reminding me that this sacred journey extended beyond my path as if the guiding energy was awakening a dormant memory—a recognition that I belonged to an unbroken lineage of seekers, warriors, and guardians who had upheld these truths across time.

I began to grasp that this sacred path was not merely about pursuing answers or striving for enlightenment as a distant ideal; it was about living in harmony with this unveiled essence and becoming a vessel through which these truths could flow into the world. Each moment of this journey felt infused with significance, as if I were preparing for a calling yet to be fully unveiled. The entire process was both humbling and exhilarating, filling me with a sense of purpose that transcended the limits of my existence.

Upon returning home, I felt an irresistible pull toward the ancient Vedic scriptures, texts that had long eluded my comprehension. Previously, I had approached the Upanishads, Bhagavad Gita, Mahabharata, and Ramayana with curiosity but struggled to grasp their depth. They seemed distant, their wisdom obscured beneath layers of abstraction. Now, a shift had occurred; these sacred texts began to resonate with me as if they awaited this moment of connection. Their teachings now appeared as living truths, awakening a sense of familiarity within me.

The fog that had obscured my perception had lifted. The verses and narratives, once dense and impenetrable, revealed themselves with remarkable clarity. Concepts such as Brahman, Atman, Maya, dharma, and moksha, which I had previously found challenging, now emerged as vivid and accessible truths. They were no longer abstract philosophies but echoes of an eternal reality I had already encountered, as if the ceremonies with Mother Ayahuasca had prepared me to finally absorb their message.

The scriptures felt more like memories to be recalled rather than lessons to be learned. The Upanishads spoke of ultimate reality—the interconnectedness of all existence. I recognized their depictions as mirroring the state of boundless consciousness I had experienced during the ceremonies. The Bhagavad Gita's call to align with one's higher purpose resonated deeply as I understood my role as a warrior on a sacred path. The Mahabharata and the Ramayana revealed themselves to be profound allegories for the divine play of creation and destruction, illustrating the eternal interplay of stillness and dynamism.

The newfound connection to Vedic wisdom was not merely an intellectual awakening; it was a profoundly emotional and spiritual experience. Each passage I read felt like a key unlocking doors within me, revealing layers of understanding long obscured. The teachings no longer felt like foreign concepts but rather intrinsic truths, as though they had always been a part of my being, waiting patiently to be rediscovered. I began to see parallels between the visions I encountered during the ceremonies and the imagery presented in the texts: the blossoming structures I perceived mirrored the metaphors of creation. The pulsating energy of the cosmos reflected the dynamic interplay of divine forces described within these scriptures.

What resonated most was the effortless harmony that emerged from everything I had encountered. It felt as if Mother Ayahuasca had intentionally led me to this moment, ensuring that I approached these texts with the reverence and openness they deserved. I no longer perceived these teachings as distant or theoretical; they transformed into vibrant, living truths resonating deeply within the core of my soul, aligning my experiences with the universal wisdom they expressed. The scriptures confirmed what I had felt, seen, and experienced, deepening my understanding of their profound significance.

The renewed awareness ignited within me a sense of awe and gratitude. It became evident that the wisdom of the Vedic texts and the insights from Mother Ayahuasca were not separate journeys but rather two manifestations of the same universal truth. Both were guiding me toward the same realization: our true nature is divine, limitless, and interconnected with all existence. As I immersed myself in these ancient teachings, I increasingly felt that my journey was part of something timeless and infinite—a play of remembrance and awakening that transcended the limitations of culture, time, and individuality.

Swami Vivekananda's reflections on Brahman, the fundamental reality of all that exists, struck a deep chord of recognition within me. Delving into his writings was akin to discovering a reflection of my journey facilitated by Mother Ayahuasca. His striking portrayal of Brahman as an infinite and timeless consciousness was not merely a philosophical idea; it resonated with a profound revelation I had experienced during one of the ceremonies.

In the depths of my connection with Mother Ayahuasca, I experienced the dissolution of the ego and the unraveling of the illusion of separation. What persisted was an infinite presence, pure and undivided, encompassing all of creation. It was timeless, spaceless, and profoundly serene, echoing precisely the descriptions offered by Swami Vivekananda and the Vedic texts. Every metaphor used to illustrate the ultimate reality—the ocean of consciousness, the formless essence, the eternal observer—aligned perfectly with the visions and feelings I experienced.

My initiation into the Vedic teachings emerged as a profound and purposeful exploration rather than a mere coincidence. An unseen hand had deliberately kept these texts from me until this crucial point in my life. In my earlier attempts, I struggled to comprehend their complexities, finding the language too abstract and the insights largely inaccessible. Following the transformative experiences granted by Mother Ayahuasca, their meanings unfolded effortlessly, as if a guiding energy had orchestrated the moment to ensure my full engagement with these teachings, free from past assumptions. Through immersive experiences during the ceremonies, Mother Ayahuasca connected me to the limitless, allowing me to see Vedic wisdom not only as theoretical concepts but also as truths to adopt.

Witnessing the harmonious convergence of these insights was truly humbling. The teachings of the ancient scriptures were not mere remnants of the past but vibrant beacons illuminating a journey I had already begun. They reinforced the lessons imparted by Mother Ayahuasca: that Brahman, the ultimate reality, is not a distant goal but the core of our being. It represents the stillness amid turmoil, the quietude beneath the noise, and the enduring essence that sustains all existence.

I recognized that the wisdom found in the Vedic texts and the teachings of Mother Ayahuasca represented two expressions of the same universal truth, steering me toward a more profound comprehension of both myself and the cosmos. My journey transformed from a quest for external answers into a celebration of the profound truths that had always resided within me, patiently awaiting my awakening.

This understanding transcended mere spirituality; it bridged the realms of mysticism and science into a cohesive framework of reality. As I reflected on my experiences, a deep curiosity drove me to explore scientific theories that sought to clarify the nature of existence. What I discovered was nothing short of remarkable: ancient wisdom and modern theoretical physics appeared to mirror one another, both pointing to the same fundamental truth, albeit through different lenses. This revelation was not isolated; many others, from both spiritual traditions and scientific communities, have converged on this same conclusion, suggesting that the boundaries between science and mysticism are not as distinct as they may seem. Whether through the teachings of ancient sages or the latest breakthroughs in quantum mechanics, the idea that consciousness and the universe are deeply interconnected is echoed in both the mystic's insights and the physicist's equations.

Whether through the teachings of ancient sages, the latest breakthroughs in quantum mechanics, or cutting-edge research in neuroscience, the idea that consciousness and the universe are deeply interconnected echoes across these diverse fields. Mystics, scientists, and neuroscientists alike have arrived at a similar conclusion, suggesting that our conscious experience is not separate from the universe but is intricately woven into its very fabric. While mystics explore this connection through spiritual practice, quantum mechanics reveals the interdependence of energy and consciousness at a subatomic level, and neuroscience delves into the brain's role in perceiving and shaping reality, all pointing toward a unified understanding of existence.

In my study of String Theory and M-theory, I encountered the Calabi-Yau manifold, a complex multidimensional construct considered integral to the universe's framework. This intricate geometry, which includes hidden dimensions, bore a striking resemblance to the floral patterns I experienced during my Ayahuasca journeys. In those transformative moments, I witnessed the universe unfolding like a series of blooming flowers, each revealing new and profound layers of reality. The vivid similarity between my visions and the Calabi-Yau manifold suggested that Mother Ayahuasca had granted me a direct and extraordinary glimpse into the underlying mathematical structure of existence.

The parallels between the membranes, or branes, in String Theory and the lokas in Vedic literature are noteworthy, bridging ancient knowledge with modern scientific paradigms. In String Theory, branes function as multidimensional planes that exist as parallel universes adjacent to our own. They are believed to encompass entire domains of existence, each characterized by unique properties intricately linked by forces beyond conventional comprehension.

Similarly, the Vedic concept of lokas represents various levels of existence, ranging from the physical to the spiritual. These lokas are not isolated realms but interconnected layers of reality that are accessible through heightened states of awareness. Both ideas propose a universe that transcends three-dimensional space, revealing a complex tapestry of parallel realities.

According to Vedic philosophy, lokas exhibit a hierarchical yet interconnected essence, with each layer denoting a specific state of awareness. This notion is akin to String Theory's claim that branes are interdependent components within a grand multidimensional framework. Just as the vibrations of strings within branes give rise to the particles and forces in our universe, the lokas in Hindu philosophy are thought to emanate from consciousness, manifesting in diverse realities.

A fascinating connection emerges within the interactions of these realms. String Theory indicates that branes can exert influence on one another through gravitational forces or quantum interactions. In a similar vein, Vedic texts suggest that lokas are interconnected, with actions in one loka echoing throughout others, thereby highlighting the inherent unity of existence despite apparent distinctions.

These comparisons unveil a key insight: reality is not a singular entity but a dynamic and intricate system of interconnected realms. Whether viewed through the scientific prism of branes or the spiritual lens of lokas, both perspectives converge on a unified truth: the universe unfolds as a multidimensional masterpiece, with each layer contributing uniquely to the expansive, cohesive whole.

Moreover, the parallel between age-old insights and modern scientific understanding transcends traditional geometric and spatial frameworks. String Theory, which illustrates the universe as being composed of vibrating strings, resonates deeply with the Hindu concept of *Nada Brahma* . This principle suggests that the cosmos emerges through sound—a harmonious tapestry of vibrations stemming from the primordial sound *OM*. Such parallels reveal that these seemingly different perspectives on the cosmos are not opposing; rather, they converge, illuminating a unified underlying reality.

The convergence of ancient wisdom and modern thought reinforces the idea that the universe is not a chaotic collection of particles but a living, coherent system guided by an underlying consciousness. Whether termed *Brahman* by sages or described as quantum fluctuations by physicists, this foundational reality serves as the source from which all arises and to which everything ultimately returns. The barriers we establish between science and spirituality, as well as between what is tangible and what is intangible, are illusions—products of our minds that vanish when confronted with profound realities.

The more deeply I engaged with my studies, the clearer the extraordinary similarities between ancient insights and modern theoretical physics became. The amplituhedron, an amazing geometric construct introduced by a renowned physicist, serves to simplify calculations within quantum field theory. Its most astonishing implication is the suggestion that space and time—the very foundations of our perceived reality—might not be the fundamental building blocks we have always presumed. Instead, space and time could be emergent features secondary to a far more profound and intricate reality. This challenges everything we have traditionally considered as truth regarding the universe, indicating that beneath the surface of space and time lies a richly layered structure that extends beyond our sensory limitations. This aligns well with the ancient wisdom advocating for unseen dimensions of reality.

Furthermore, this groundbreaking perspective intertwines seamlessly with Vedic teachings on *Maya*, illustrating that the material world we perceive is an elaborate illusion. This veil masks the fundamental truth of existence. The Vedas assert that what we contemplate as space, time, and form is merely a mirage projected by our limited senses onto the canvas of ultimate consciousness. Ancient sages conveyed this illusory essence of the world millennia ago, declaring that the only true reality is Brahman, the Absolute, unchanging consciousness that underpins all existence.

The amplituhedron embodies ancient wisdom through the contemporary language of theoretical physics. If space and time are not fundamental pillars, then our understanding of the universe becomes a mesmerizing projection—an alluring façade emerging from a profoundly deeper reality. My visions resonate with this transformative scientific perspective: a universe that transcends static three-dimensional confines, creating an intricate tapestry of interconnections and possibilities stemming from an essence that defies physical characterization.

In addition, the beauty of the amplituhedron as a mathematical structure evokes the inherent perfection of nature's design—a pattern I glimpsed during the ceremonies in the fractal-like unfoldings and infinite layers of reality. The universe is not a random accident but a harmonious, purposeful system guided by a superintelligence far beyond the reach of modern science. This superintelligence, as the ancient sages described, is the ultimate reality, the essence from which all things arise and to which all things eventually return.

The connections continued to deepen. The mathematical assertion that space and time are not fundamental prompts a crucial inquiry: If they are not at the core of reality, then what is? Modern scientific research, Vedic teachings, and my Ayahuasca experiences converge on the same conclusion: consciousness. It is not that consciousness springs from the brain or the material universe; instead, the physical universe manifests within consciousness. This inversion of viewpoint aligns with what the amplituhedron implies: a universe constructed not on material foundations but emerging from a deeper, unified field of existence.

This acknowledgment brings forth another question that science grapples with: What constitutes matter? As we delve deeper into the essence of matter, it becomes increasingly elusive. Subatomic particles vanish into fields of probability or waves of energy when scrutinized closely. They are not solid objects but dynamic events within an expanse of limitless potential. The Vedic sages recognized this as well, asserting that what we perceive as concrete, tangible matter is merely a play of consciousness—an energetic dance that appears real yet possesses no independent existence. Mother Ayahuasca unveiled this play with vivid clarity, dissolving the confines of my perception and presenting the universe as a wave in an ocean of consciousness.

Reflecting on these interconnections, it becomes clear that ancient sages and modern scientists have explored the same enigmas from diverse perspectives. Sages utilize meditation, intuition, and direct experience to unveil existential truths, while scientists rely on mathematics, experimentation, and hypotheses. Nevertheless, both paths ultimately converge on the same realization: the universe is far more mysterious and awe-inspiring than our everyday experiences tend to reveal, and it is consciousness—rather than matter—that holds foundational significance.

The convergence of the amplituhedron, M-theory, ancient Vedic wisdom, and my Ayahuasca experiences aligns with the groundbreaking work of many other reputable scientists who have explored the idea that the universe is not as it seems. Various theories suggest that what we perceive as reality may not be a fundamental truth at all. Some propose that the universe is a vast, intricate simulation, a projection of higher-dimensional information, or even a hologram. These ideas challenge the conventional understanding of space and time, indicating that our physical world might be an illusion—a complex, dynamic illusion shaped by the consciousness that permeates everything.

Studies in quantum mechanics and cosmology point to the possibility that the fabric of reality is far more malleable and interconnected than previously imagined.

Furthermore, these theories suggest that consciousness is the true essence of existence and that the physical world is merely a projection, akin to the holographic universe theory, in which everything we see is a reflection of deeper, unseen layers of reality. The idea that our universe is not "real" in the traditional sense but rather a constructed experience of consciousness has become a fascinating point of intersection between science and spirituality. This concept reinforces the notion that we, as conscious beings, are not separate from the cosmos but integral to its unfolding. Our awareness shapes and reflects the universe, suggesting that we are not merely participants in the cosmic dance but are the very source and expression of it.

The enigmatic "hard problem of consciousness," which concerns how subjective experiences arise from physical interactions, underwent a profound shift following my Ayahuasca experiences. The ceremonies stripped away the veil of perceived reality, positioning consciousness not merely as a byproduct of brain activity but as the fundamental cornerstone of existence—the source from which the universe unfolds. I realized that genuine investigation should focus not on the characteristics of consciousness but on the intrinsic nature of matter itself.

Reflecting on my experiences revealed that the core inquiry is not how consciousness emerges from the material world but rather how our understanding of matter is shaped by consciousness. My Ayahuasca experience demonstrated that the material world lacks the permanence and stability we often attribute to it. As I sought to comprehend my interpretation of reality, it shifted into pure energy and vibrations, eventually settling into profound, serene stillness. The physical forms with which I once identified were merely ephemeral imprints on the surface of a vast, eternal truth.

This insight aligns with the teachings of ancient Vedic philosophies, which describe the material world as Maya—an illusion born from the interplay of consciousness. According to the sages, our perception of the physical world is akin to a fleeting wave on the vast, infinite ocean of awareness. During my Ayahuasca ceremonies, the "wave" of the physical universe dissolved, leaving only the boundless, ever-present consciousness from which all existence emerges.

Modern physics also points to this same enigma. As I explored the essence of matter through scientific investigation, I understood that what we label as "matter" becomes increasingly elusive upon deeper scrutiny. At the atomic level, solid constructs dissolve into fundamental particles, which consist primarily of empty space. At the subatomic level, particles dissipate into spectrums of probabilities and waveforms—transient energy patterns that manifest more as events than as concrete entities. Delving even further, these waveforms dissolve into fields, vibrations, and relationships. Ultimately, even the notion of "something" fades, leaving only a faint trace of existence.

The investigation into the fundamental nature of matter parallels my spiritual journey. The revelations experienced during the ceremonies shed light on the cutting edge of scientific understanding. The material world, previously viewed as rigid and fixed, unfolds as a dynamic interplay of energy steered by unseen forces. The ancient Vedic sages depicted this interplay as *Lila* , the divine enactment of creation, in which limitless consciousness takes shape in countless forms, only to withdraw them back into its essence.

Thus, the proper inquiry becomes: What is matter if not the projection of consciousness itself? Mother Ayahuasca revealed that everything I once considered "real"—the body, the mind, and even the cosmos—was nothing more than a transient reflection of something far more profound. The physical realm is not the foundation; it is an illusion. It is not the cause but the effect—a projection of consciousness vibrating at different frequencies to create the appearance of form and solidity. Matter, in its essence, is not real; it is a fleeting manifestation of awareness, a temporary expression of the boundless consciousness that transcends it all. The galaxies, the planets, the stars, and even my physical form blend into manifestations of the same limitless consciousness. We are not apart from the universe; we are its origin, the boundless awareness from which all creation springs. Everything that exists is a reflection of consciousness, a dynamic expression unfolding from within.

This understanding radically reframes the scientific pursuit of the "hard problem of consciousness." Consciousness is not a phenomenon needing explanation; it is the very foundation upon which all explanations stand. It is the context from which all inquiries arise and within which all answers reside. The true challenge lies in comprehending how this infinite, unbounded awareness manifests as the multitude of forms we label as reality. The Vedic teachings offer a profound resolution to this mystery: It is all *Lila* , the eternal play of consciousness, that creates, sustains, and ultimately dissolves the illusion of the material world.

One of the most powerful revelations I had was that my daughter embodies the spirit of my mother. This felt both incredible and profoundly affirming. From the moment she was born, I could feel this connection. The light in her eyes reminded me of my mother's spirit, and I knew in my heart that this bond was real. This realization transcended logic; it was a deep, undeniable awareness. I also came to understand that her mother carried the energy of Goddess Kali, known for fierce protection and powerful creation. Ma Kali's essence dissolves illusions and reveals profound truths, and witnessing this in my daughter's mother shifted how I viewed our connection. It became evident that our relationship wasn't just shaped by experiences but by a sacred exchange of energy. The energy I possess, although yet to be fully revealed, was harmonized with the energy of Ma Kali and poised for its emergence. This realization made me understand that creation and destruction are inseparable and that both are essential energies in the ongoing process of growth and transformation.

As these revelations unfolded, the universe revealed its elaborate architecture, illustrating how every thread of life is interconnected. Each relationship, encounter, and even challenge is part of an immense design—a divine tapestry woven with care. These connections were not mere coincidences; they were intentional and meaningful, forming a cosmic order that transcended my understanding. It was a humbling realization to witness how intricately my existence intertwined with the eternal truths of the cosmos. I felt a profound reverence for the unseen energy guiding my journey toward these significant truths, coupled with a great sense of responsibility. These revelations were no ordinary knowledge to be passively acknowledged or filed away; they called for action, urging me to embody them in every aspect of my life.

A persistent thought, quietly guided by Mother Ayahuasca, echoed in my mind, urging me to reflect on something beyond the laws and rules that often govern our spiritual pursuits. She impressed upon me that there are no strict commandments like those etched in stone; instead, there is only one fundamental requirement for enlightenment:

Do No Harm.

This truth isn't about following rigid moral laws or adhering to prescribed dogmas; it is a simple yet profound principle—one that requires us to engage with the world and with ourselves in a way that honors life in all its forms. It isn't just about refraining from causing harm; it is about actively cultivating compassion, respect, and reverence for the interconnectedness of all beings.

In this realization, Mother Ayahuasca revealed the essence of spiritual awakening: true enlightenment lies in the absence of harm. This isn't just about avoiding violence or inflicting harm on others; it extends to the way we treat ourselves. The same compassion and understanding that we extend to others must also be directed inward, acknowledging the sacredness of our being. I realized that each moment of harmful thought, word, or action—no matter how small—creates ripples that disrupt the flow of peace and unity, which is our natural state. By choosing not to harm, we align ourselves with the deep, cosmic flow of Love and Oneness that permeates all existence. This principle doesn't require complex understanding or the memorization of rules; it simply requires us to be present, to be aware of our impact on the world, and to choose actions born from love, not fear.

Ma Kali's fierce protection and destruction are about dissolving the illusions that separate us from this essential truth. She embodies the destructive force needed to tear down the barriers of ignorance and fear and, in doing so, reveals the peaceful, compassionate nature that lies beneath. Understanding this, I recognized that my role in this life was to honor this sacred principle of non-harm and to contribute to the healing and harmony of all beings. This profound internal shift further solidified my understanding that the universe isn't a place of chaos but rather one of profound order, where every living being plays an essential role in sustaining balance.

The lessons became evident: my purpose was not to preach or teach but to fully integrate these revelations into my life, allowing them to transform the way I live, love, and engage with the world. This sense of responsibility was not a burden; it was liberating. It filled my life with a sense of direction and clarity previously unknown to me. The wisdom I received was not for my own sake; it was a treasure meant to be shared—a vibrant energy to be conveyed through love, compassion, and understanding. It called me to align my life with the divine structure I had witnessed and to honor the interconnectedness of all beings by living in harmony with that truth. In this awakened understanding, I envisioned myself as both a bridge and a vessel—connecting the earthly with the Divine and channeling these universal truths into the world. My experiences, relationships, and challenges were integral to this sacred purpose. Although my journey was far from complete, I carried a heightened sense of direction, aware that each step was guided by a reality far greater than myself.

Nearly a year and a half after my second retreat at Nimea Kaya Sanctuary, I felt the unmistakable call of Mother Ayahuasca once more. Her presence was undeniable, and her voice was clear and insistent, summoning me to continue the journey I had begun. This call felt different; it bore a gravity and solemnity that coursed through my soul as if the universe itself were extending an invitation I could neither ignore nor postpone.

My journey would lead me to Spirit Quest Sanctuary—an esteemed location renowned for its healing and transformative depth, even though it had always seemed just beyond my reach. This calling carried an urgency; it suggested that this was not merely a continuation of my journey but a pivotal evolution. I sensed that this journey would redefine my path, for the stakes were raised, the lessons would be deeper, and the responsibilities weightier. Mother Ayahuasca's presence would not be playful this time; it would be resolute. "You are prepared," she seemed to convey, her voice resonating in the quiet of my meditations.

As I contemplated my return to the Amazon, a mix of anticipation and anxiety coursed through me.

There was excitement about what Spirit Quest Sanctuary would offer and a readiness to delve into deeper mysteries, yet there was also apprehension. I understood this journey would require more of me than ever before. It was not simply about healing or comprehension but rather about fully embracing the truths I had glimpsed and weaving them into the fabric of my existence.

Even before I set foot in Spirit Quest Sanctuary, I sensed its significance. The name carried a weight of reverence; it represented not just a physical location but also a state of being—a place where the veil between the physical and the spiritual thins, allowing for interaction with the Absolute. I had heard tales of the sanctuary: its profound ceremonial practices led by gifted shamans, the sacred jungle surrounding it, and the transformations it catalyzed in those who entered its embrace. The very thought of stepping into this sacred space filled me with awe and a deep sense of destiny.

However, I recognized that this preparation required a new approach. The journey ahead called for more than mere physical readiness; it necessitated a cleansing of both body and mind. I felt a primal urge to align myself with the energies I would soon encounter. The months leading up to the retreat became a deliberate period of preparation. I changed my diet, engaged in daily meditation, and eliminated distractions to create room for introspection. I honored my body as a temple, nourishing it with wholesome foods and abstaining from anything that might cloud my clarity. This process transcended discipline; it was an act of devotion—an offering to the sacred journey that awaited me.

Fasting became a critical aspect of this preparation —not as deprivation but as a means of resetting and tuning my body to the finer energies I would soon encounter. Meditation became my foundation, a ritual anchoring me in the present moment. Each session felt like peeling away another layer, revealing the raw essence of my inner self. I focused on my breath, the stillness within, and nurturing a sense of openness and receptivity. The more I meditated, the more palpable the transformation became—a subtle yet profound shift in my awareness.

Mentally, I plunged inward, using introspection to scrutinize my fears, desires, and attachments. I journaled daily, pouring my thoughts and emotions onto the pages before me. This practice acted as a mirror, reflecting the patterns and beliefs that no longer served me. I viewed this preparatory period as an opportunity to shed the burdens I had carried —emotional weights, unresolved questions, and lingering doubts—so that I could enter the retreat feeling free and light.

Spiritually, I immersed myself in practices that deepened my connection to the Divine. I sought solace in nature, walking in silence and marveling at the intricate beauty surrounding me. The rustling leaves, the chirping birds, and the gentle whisper of the wind reminded me of the sacredness present in all things. I delved into spiritual literature, drawing inspiration from the wisdom of those who had traversed this path before me. Every word and every verse felt like a thread, drawing me closer to the infinite.

This preparation transcended mere necessity; it evolved into a profound commitment. Each act of cleansing and introspection signified a commitment—a way of communicating to the universe that I was ready to surrender, receive, and transform. I approached this process with reverence, understanding that the depth of my preparation would shape the profundity of my experience. The journey ahead demanded my unwavering commitment and presence, and I resolved to invest my entire being in it.

As days passed, I could feel the transformation taking root within me. My mind quieted, my body lightened, and my spirit resonated more finely. The clarity and focus I cultivated during this time became a solid foundation for what lay ahead. The journey to Spirit Quest Sanctuary was not merely a destination; it was a call to step into a higher version of myself, prepared to embrace the mysteries and insights awaiting my arrival.

As I packed my belongings, memories and lessons from Nimea Kaya Sanctuary and the Sacred Valley filled my thoughts. Each item folded into my bag was filled with significance—a piece of the story leading me to this moment. This act was not routine; it became a ritual of preparation and a mindful acknowledgment of the path I was about to embark upon.

I felt like a warrior donning sacred armor—not for traditional battle, but for an encounter that would test my spirit rather than my strength. The tools I carried were not weapons but insights: the resilience I had cultivated, the revelations I had gleaned, and the deep sense of unity I had experienced with the universe through Mother Ayahuasca. My armor was my willingness to embrace truth, my readiness to surrender, and my trust in the journey unfolding before me. The question that had loomed over me—"Who am I?"—had shifted in weight and significance. It no longer weighed me down as a burden but instead emerged as a guiding light, gently nudging me toward clarity. This question transformed from an obstacle into an ally, urging me to embrace the mysteries and forge ahead with courage and curiosity.

The heart of the Amazon awaited, pulsating with ancient wisdom and wild beauty. I felt that this journey would encompass more than a physical exploration; it would deepen the spiritual quest ignited years ago. I stood ready to embrace the unknown, prepared to encounter whatever truths and revelations Mother Ayahuasca had in store for me. The path unfolded before me, glowing with potential, and with every fiber of my being, I felt prepared to take the next step.

On the day of my departure for Spirit Quest, eagerness filled my mind. Every step toward the sanctuary was intentional, with each mile shedding the old to make way for the new. As the plane soared over the sprawling jungle, I surrendered deeply. I was no longer the individual who had entered Nimea Kaya Sanctuary years earlier. I had glimpsed the infinite, been touched by the Divine, and now bore the responsibility of embodying those truths.

This was far more than just another retreat; it was a homecoming. It marked a call to wholeheartedly embrace transformation and to step into the depths of my true self. The journey to Spirit Quest transcended physicality; it symbolized the continuation of a sacred odyssey—one that would shape the core of my being.

This insight transformed my understanding of existence. If the universe is merely a wave in the vast ocean of consciousness, then the essence of all things is inherently spiritual. This understanding carries profound implications, revealing that the separations we perceive—the divides between self and other, mind and body, spirit and material—are merely illusions stemming from a limited perspective. At the heart of it all, everything is interconnected, with one consciousness manifesting in infinite forms.

Chapter Ten

Unveiling the Lord Shiva

The journey to Spirit Quest Sanctuary commenced with an awe-inspiring view of the Amazon River, winding gracefully through a vibrant green jungle. The river, expansive and powerful, seemed to stretch into infinity, its surface shimmering as sunlight danced across it. As the boat glided through the water, the surrounding jungle pulsed with life, its dense greenery vibrant with energy. Each bend of the river unveiled a fresh aspect of nature's magnificence: towering trees with leaves glimmering in various shades of green, occasional splashes of colorful flowers, and the distant calls of unseen wildlife echoing from the depths of the forest. The air, saturated with moisture and earthy aromas, enveloped me in a sense of entering a realm preserved in time.

The thirty-minute boat ride from Iquitos felt dreamlike, suggesting that the separation between the lively city and this untouched paradise was both physical and spiritual. As the boat rocked gently in the current, I sank deeper into the beauty surrounding me. The dense jungle whispered age-old secrets, creating an atmosphere of awe and reverence. The trees seemed to share their knowledge, offering wisdom to anyone willing to listen. The steady flow of the river served as a soothing backdrop, encouraging me to pause, reflect, and fully immerse myself in the moment. An unmistakable tension hung in the air; something transformative loomed on the horizon beyond my current comprehension.

Upon stepping into the sanctuary, a profound sense of belonging enveloped me. The moment my feet connected with the earth, I felt an intense bond with the place, as if I had returned home after a long journey. The sacred land welcomed me, and the jungle's energy blanketed me like a comforting embrace. This was not merely a physical retreat; the sanctuary resonated with spiritual vibrations that permeated the very soil. It felt alive, its roots intertwined with the earth, and its heart synchronized with the jungle's pulse. I sensed the presence of the ancients here, their wisdom embedded in the ground beneath me.

The intoxicating scents of damp earth and blooming flowers intensified the allure of this sacred locale. Each breath felt deeper and more significant as I inhaled the spirit of the jungle. The flowers, radiant and vibrant, released their essence into the atmosphere, crafting a fragrant symphony that anchored me in the present. The river murmured a melodic welcome, its gentle current echoing the cycles of life that began in this interconnected space. This was far more than a simple retreat; it was a reconnection to something primal, something eternal. Here, time blurred, leaving only the profound essence of the land, the river, and the spirits of the jungle. This felt like home.

I reunited with my spiritual brother from India, whose presence had been revealed to me by Mother Ayahuasca as my past lifetime teacher during my second retreat at Nimea Kaya. The moment we met, an intense feeling of familiarity sparked between us, erasing any doubts about the distance or time apart. His grounding presence initiated a moment of shared understanding as we recognized that our destinies were intertwined for a reason, woven together through the sacred teachings bestowed upon us. The joy of our reconnection radiated in the air, infused with the warmth of a shared history, both familiar and mysterious. Our bond, cultivated through our unique journeys, felt like a powerful energy, drawing us closer as we prepared for the imminent challenges and insights that awaited us.

We decided to fast during the Ayahuasca ceremonies, a commitment that transcended mere dietary choices. The fast was a sacred practice, a collective experience designed to strengthen our connection and sharpen our intentions. We agreed to consume only revitalizing juices, allowing our bodies and minds to cleanse and prepare for the sacred ceremonies ahead. Fasting became a form of devotion, an offering not only to the gods and goddesses but also to Mother Ayahuasca, whom we were about to encounter. It represented purification, laying the groundwork for significant transformation. In the quiet of fasting, we discovered clarity, increased sensitivity to the surrounding energies, and a growing sense of anticipation with each passing day.

Our path would guide us through ten sacred encounters with the spirits of the holy plants, each serving as a ceremonial step toward deeper understanding and awakening. Ayahuasca, Huachuma, Bobinsana, and tobacco ceremonies would lead us into realms beyond our usual perception, challenging the limits of self-awareness. Each ceremony invited us to confront and let go of the illusions that had confined us while unearthing buried truths. The potential inherent in the sacred medicines instilled in us a profound sense of gratitude. We recognized that every experience would serve as a gateway to healing, growth, and the revelation of long-hidden mysteries.

As we stood together in silent acknowledgment of the sacred path ahead, I felt the gravity of the commitment we had undertaken. This was a pilgrimage, a transformative journey demanding significant inner work. We were not present merely to receive; we were here to dedicate ourselves—our hearts, minds, and souls—to the teachings of the plant medicines and the distilled wisdom of the jungle. The weight of this commitment was both humbling and empowering, heralding the commencement of our profound journey together as spiritual brothers traversing the portals of the unknown.

That night, as darkness cloaked the sky, the first ceremony began, shrouded in a tension that electrified the atmosphere. The energy around us vibrated like a sentient being, and the jungle seemed to hold its breath in reverence, awaiting the sacred event. The symphony of the rainforest softened, revealing only the distant hum of life and the gentle rustling of leaves. The maloca, our ceremonial haven, flickered with candlelight, casting golden shadows that danced along the wooden beams, filling the space with the energy of the gathering. The candle flames flickered softly, illuminating the varied expressions of the participants—some anxious, others serene—but all united in a shared purpose. The air was charged with sacredness, brimming with possibility.

Four shamans—two men and two women—stood poised, embodying an intense serenity. They exuded a timeless wisdom that was both profoundly ingrained and instinctive. Their presence conveyed a blend of power and elegance, akin to guardians who had conducted these sacred rituals for countless generations. Their energy felt boundless, grounding the ceremony in a hallowed reality that transcended ordinary existence. Every gesture of the shamans was deliberate, as though the ceremony had been kindled in their spirits long before anyone consumed the holy medicine.

As the ritual began, the shamans took their positions, initiating their sacred chants. Their icaros gradually filled the maloca, starting softly and quickly rising to powerful resonance, infusing the atmosphere with age-old enchantment. The songs exuded a rich, vibrant energy, evoking a deep connection with the earth beneath us. Their voices, both ethereal and soothing, infiltrated the core of my being. Each note acted as a beacon, guiding us into dimensions beyond ordinary reality and the constraints of time. The ceremony unfolded organically, with the consistent cadence of the icaros forming a protective barrier for the experience to come.

I found myself relaxing as my senses heightened, each moment pregnant with suspense. The maloca radiated sacredness and embraced us in a silence that demanded reverence, calling us to prepare for the journey ahead. The air hung thick with the aroma of burning incense and sacred herbs, adding another dimension of grounding to the experience. The jungle, the shamans, and the energy of the ceremony fused into a singular, living entity. The imminence of the experience was tangible, guiding us toward the unknown with love, trust, and deep respect for the teachings that were about to unfold.

I ingested a larger quantity of Ayahuasca than I was used to consuming in a single serving at Nimea Kaya. The bitter taste served as a familiar reminder of the medicine's potency. As the minutes passed, I sensed a transformation. The symphony of the jungle intensified as the night deepened. The eerie calls of nocturnal animals reverberated through the encroaching darkness, each note pulsating with primal energy. The hum of insects formed a rhythmic composition, as though an invisible orchestra had tuned in for a performance that only the jungle could comprehend. Leaves rustled softly in the night breeze, whispering secrets while the distant croaks of frogs intertwined like melodies. All sounds merged, crafting an otherworldly harmony that was both enchanting and alive, as if the jungle itself were a conscious entity serenading us in this sacred space. The flickering candle flames seemed to pulse with an incomprehensible rhythm, their light sparkling with a magical essence.

The shamans' voices flowed through the darkness, carrying an age-old power that resonated throughout the maloca. Their sound was entwined with the rhythmic shaking of the chakapa leaves, producing an almost hypnotic cadence that reverberated within the space. Their icaros brought solace and authority, igniting something deep within me and drawing me toward a realm that transcended ordinary perception. As the shamans navigated the maloca, their voices centered on each participant, with each note infused with sacred intention, gently opening the crown chakra of everyone in the circle.

As the vibrant energy of their icaros wrapped around me, reality underwent a noticeable transformation. The familiar environment of the maloca began to fade, blending like colors on an artist's palette. The warmth of the room, the heaviness of the air, and the flickering candlelight dissipated, unveiling a realm that felt both alien and dreamlike. To my astonishment, I found myself resting on an invisible surface, the sensation of weightlessness washing over me. My essence, liberated from the maloca and earthly limitations, drifted in a transcendent sphere. I had been transported to a realm where the fundamental principles of existence diverged from anything I had previously known.

The atmosphere in this unfamiliar space felt unnervingly sterile as if I had crossed into a realm devoid of nature, where organic life had yielded to an artificial, almost lifeless presence. The air was stripped of warmth and scent; it felt cold and clinical, lacking any trace of human warmth. There was no comfort, no grounding energy from the surrounding jungle—only an unnatural silence. I sensed that I was being prepared for an unknown surgical operation—my very essence scrutinized beneath the unforgiving glow of this alien operating hangar.

The sensation was disorienting as if I were suspended between two worlds—neither entirely in the maloca nor completely anchored in this foreign space. A strange detachment from my body engulfed me, making it feel as if it belonged to someone else. Each passing moment amplified my awareness of external forces much stronger than my own, yet, strangely, I felt no anxiety—only a profound sense of surrender. I understood that this unfolding experience was mine to embrace, a significant moment in my journey, though its entire meaning remained out of reach.

Out of nowhere, two tiny robot-like beings materialized in the sterile, alien environment. No taller than two feet, their metallic forms shone in the peculiar light flooding the room. Their movements were meticulous and calculated, mechanical in every regard, as if each action had been programmed and rehearsed for a singular purpose. They emitted no warmth or emotion, only an unsettling, clinical detachment as they approached their task, indifferent to the living being before them.

Suspended just above me, they hovered with an unsettling stillness, their presence observing me with an intensity that felt unnaturally distant. There was no hint of curiosity in their gaze; instead, it exuded efficiency, singularly focused on their assignment. Each movement exhibited such precision that they seemed to operate outside the boundaries of space and time. They appeared to be advanced beings conducting a profound exploration into the nature of my existence. Without warning, they reached toward me, their motion so fluid and instantaneous that I barely had time to comprehend the event before they extracted genetic material from me.

The process brought no discomfort; instead, there was a clinical awareness that something vital had been drawn from me. It was not physical pain but rather a subtle loss, as if a very tiny part of me had been removed. This feeling settled into my awareness—not as an alarm but as acknowledgment. It was a knowing that this act was part of a cosmic orchestration, a journey of which I was a part yet could not fully understand. It felt like a necessary chapter in my journey, shrouded in meaning I could not grasp at that moment.

Just as swiftly as they had appeared, the entities vanished into the very emptiness from which they had emerged. Their departure was as silent and rapid as their arrival, leaving behind a void filled with lingering disorientation. I remained in a strange limbo, barely grasping the events that had unfolded yet accepting them with a sense of eerie calm. All I could do was yield to this experience, allowing the disorienting energy to settle within me as I played a role in a vast, intricate tapestry.

The shamans continued their work, moving with unwavering determination from one individual to the next, their presence a steadying force. When they reached an elderly woman seated opposite me, a shocking transformation erupted. She emitted guttural, beast-like growls that shattered the stillness, piercing the air with a ferocity unlike anything I had ever encountered. The sound was indescribable: primal, savage, and otherworldly. It was as though an ancient malevolence had seized her essence, turning her voice into a conduit for something dark. The noise reverberated through the space like a violent storm—a deep, throbbing force that quickened my heartbeat and sent chills creeping beneath my skin. Each wail tore through the air with tremendous strength as if the walls of the maloca trembled in response.

The intensity of her roars sent a surge of dread coursing through my being. Her voice echoed the torment of a soul caught in turbulent realms. The atmosphere thickened with oppressive darkness, and her voice became the channel through which that darkness poured forth. I sensed the heavy weight of this malevolent energy creeping across the room, casting shadows around everyone present. My body tensed involuntarily—a reflexive response to the sheer horror of the sounds emanating from her—and I found myself unable to avert my gaze, captivated by the chaotic energy engulfing her.

Undeterred by the terrifying spectacle, the shamans rallied around her with renewed urgency. Their icaros grew louder and more compelling, forged into a protective barrier against the dark energy seeking to consume the woman. The songs sharpened; each note became a weapon crafted to vanquish the horror unfolding before us. The ceremony intensified as their voices echoed through the maloca, each sound a reverberation within the sacred space—a call to expel the darkness. It became a battle of sound overcoming shadow, the strength of their songs striving to reclaim the light threatened by the consuming darkness. I felt the combined energy of the shamans and participants coalescing, pushing back against the force that had seized her so violently.

At that moment, the true power of the shamans' icaros became apparent. They were more than just songs; they were weapons, shields, and ancient rituals fashioned to confront the darkness that sometimes erupted during these profound spiritual journeys. The energy in the maloca transformed as their voices tore through the weighty atmosphere, carrying with them the wisdom and strength of centuries. Their icaros were potent instruments of light designed to dispel forces that sought to invade and corrupt. Every note they sang was woven into the fabric of the universe, drawing away the darkness inch by inch.

Suddenly, a wave of nausea swept over me, sending my body into convulsions as I leaned over my purge bucket. The room spiraled around me, and my stomach churned with turmoil. This was not mere physical sickness; it was an overwhelming wave of malevolent energy crashing over me. A sinister voice echoed in my mind, icy and relentless, sending shivers through my core: "You will die! You will die!" This cruel, sinister voice, smiling as it spoke, repeated its deadly refrain with such force that it seemed to tear at the fabric of reality. Panic gripped the edges of my mind, threatening to swallow me whole, but I focused all my energy on grounding myself.

In that fearful space, I managed to utter, "If I die, so be it." A peculiar tranquility washed over me—a profound acceptance of whatever lay ahead on this journey. The voice persisted, "You will die!" Its grip tightened with a frigid reminder of impending doom, yet I refused to capitulate. Darkness, that malevolent force, sought to infiltrate my being, aiming to consume me whole, but I resisted.

Instead of surrendering to fear, I summoned a greater force: Love.

With my face pressed into the bucket, I concentrated all my energy on emanating pure, unconditional love. I directed it toward the woman still wracked with torment, as well as toward the entity plaguing her. The more love I projected, the more palpable the energy shift became. Love emerged as the strongest force at my disposal. The dark presence began to wane in its wake, unable to withstand the purity of my intentions. I continued to send forth love, saturating the space with it and refusing to allow fear to dominate. The purging culminated, reaching a nearly unbearable intensity; each ounce of darkness within me was expelled as though something vile had anchored itself deep within me. My body shook with effort as I wrestled with this ancient, sinister presence that clung to me with oppressive weight.

Mother Ayahuasca's voice returned—calm yet resolute—a guiding hand through the turmoil. "You must purge this darkness completely," she instructed her words a beacon amid the chaos. This was the only path forward, and there was no time for hesitation. I fought with every sinew of my being, every muscle straining against the vile energy. My stomach twisted violently as I felt myself being torn apart from within, but I pressed on, steadfast in my determination to expel every bit of whatever this darkness was.

A fierce explosion of dark energy erupted from my core as if a dam had burst, releasing a torrent that cascaded through my being. I felt the shadows surge from within me like a relentless flood, dissolving into the purifying vessel prepared to receive them. A wave of relief swept over me, and a profound calmness engulfed my entire being, infusing me with a deep sense of serenity.

The woman, once engulfed in torment, now lay in tranquil stillness, her body at rest and her suffering seemingly lifted. The atmosphere in the maloca transformed, enshrouding the space in a profound and respectful hush. Outside, the jungle paused in reverence for the healing that had taken place. Anxiety dissipated, replaced by the calming silence that followed the earlier turmoil.

Mother Ayahuasca spoke once again, her voice steady yet infused with profound insight. She revealed that I had been guided to Spirit Quest for this singular purpose, articulating that every event leading to this moment had been orchestrated by a greater divine design. She reminded me of the time, four years prior, when my attempts to reach Spirit Quest had been thwarted, explaining that I had not yet been prepared—either spiritually or physically. Vital lessons remained unlearned, and necessary purifications awaited. I had to cleanse my mind and body before fully stepping into the sacred space of healing that had summoned me here.

The weight of her revelations reverberated through me, piercing deep into my essence. I understood that the journey I had undertaken was not merely about the ceremonies themselves but about peeling away the layers of illusion, confronting old scars, and clearing the path to my true self. It wasn't a matter of transforming into someone else; it was about shedding the false layers that had obscured my essence all along. Only by revealing the truth of who I truly was could I fully appreciate the profound gifts that Spirit Quest Sanctuary had to offer. The wisdom imparted over the past four years —the retreats, the cleansing—had orchestrated my arrival at this pivotal moment of spiritual readiness.

Mother Ayahuasca expanded on the profound role of the shamans, who transcended the role of mere guides. Their sacred mission involved fostering each individual's communion with the Divine. Acting as conduits between our physical world and the spiritual dimension, they navigated us through our transformative processes, steering us toward enlightenment. Each participant arriving at Spirit Quest carried a divine blueprint, embarking on a distinctive path toward higher realms of existence. The shamans bore the sacred responsibility of equipping us to encounter the Divine, assisting in dismantling the obstacles that obscured our authentic selves.

As her words echoed in my mind, clarity wrapped around me like a warm embrace. The essence of my healing transformed from an individual experience into a collective journey of metamorphosis. The work undertaken not only that night but in every ceremony and ritual contributed to a larger narrative of spiritual evolution. I felt deeply honored to partake in this sacred ceremony, my heart swelling with gratitude as I recognized the continuous guidance of the Divine.

A profound metamorphosis awakened within me, subtly revealing itself in the deepest corners of my soul. Looking down at myself, I marveled at what I saw: a flowing, long white ceremonial robe illuminated by flecks of gold, reflecting golden light throughout the maloca. Strangely, there was no candlelight in the space at that moment, yet the garment glowed with an ethereal brilliance. This peculiar robe, which I had brought with me driven by an inexplicable need, seemed woven to resonate with the sacred energy now flowing through me. It was as though I had instinctively prepared for this crucial moment, unaware of its true significance.

Adorning my forehead was the Tripundra, a sacred symbol of Lord Shiva, consisting of three horizontal lines of holy ash topped with a vertical red stripe—a testament to my devotion and recognition of my spiritual bond. A powerful instinct had compelled me to carry the ash, which now manifested as a profound affirmation of my transformative path—a clear indication that I was unveiling something far greater than my previous self. Every symbol and element harmoniously converged, revealing an undeniable truth that could no longer be ignored.

The voice of Mother Ayahuasca surrounded me once more, emanating a profound sense of warmth, pride, and acknowledgment. She proclaimed, "You are Shiva." Her declaration echoed throughout my entire being, banishing all doubts and uncertainties; I was aligned with the divine presence that had always resided within me. She instructed, "There is no need to bow before the shamans. Simply honor them with folded hands, for they are presenting to you every soul present for absolution." Having transcended the need for external validation, I embraced my authentic self—an energy that soared beyond ego and self-imposed limitations.

This liberation felt overwhelming. It wasn't arrogance or pride that filled me, but a profound understanding and peace. I recognized that I was part of an eternal cycle entwined with the divine rhythm of the universe. I was Shiva, the embodiment of unyielding awareness and infinite energy, and through this realization, I felt the vast consciousness permeating the cosmos surging within me. The sacred rituals, the enchanting icaros sung by the shamans, the self-sacrifice, and the presence of Mother Ayahuasca guided me to this critical juncture, marking my role as a vital contributor to the cosmic symphony of existence.

With a more solemn tone, Mother Ayahuasca elaborated on the nature of the malignant energy I had confronted. It was an Asura, a formidable demon tethered to the woman for eons, feeding off her despair and agony. This dark entity, having traversed countless lifetimes, infiltrated the sacred space we occupied, seeking to disrupt our harmony. Its primary objective was Selva, the embodiment of Shakti energy and the Divine Mother. In its ravenous pursuit of control, the demon sought to overwhelm her energy and invade the sanctity of our gathering.

As her words settled in, a tunnel of radiant light appeared above the altar, pulsating with undeniable warmth and power, resembling a portal that bridged realms. From within the glowing passage, a procession of celestial beings emerged, their serene and authoritative presence commanding the space. They announced the arrival of Don Howard with a quiet reverence that felt both ancient and timeless. At the forefront of this procession, jester-like figures danced, their voices carrying through the air as they loudly proclaimed, "Don Howard is coming! Don Howard is coming!" The golden chariot that followed gleamed with divine radiance; its brilliance was overwhelming, and the air around it seemed to crackle with sacred energy.

The vibrations pulsed through my body, heightening the sense that something monumental was unfolding before me. I stood motionless, overwhelmed by the feeling that the entire universe was converging in this single, breathless moment. The door of the chariot slowly creaked open, yet, to my astonishment, no one emerged. The chariot remained empty, its radiant light casting an ethereal glow into the stillness around it. An unspoken sense of wonder gripped me, mingling with a quiet, profound question. Without thinking, I asked, "Where is Don Howard?"

With a gentle, knowing smile, Mother Ayahuasca answered, "Did you expect his physical form? He is everywhere, safeguarding this sanctuary and his most cherished treasure—his daughter, Selva." Her statement resonated with profound truth, revealing that Don Howard was not bound by physical existence; his spirit, energy, and love for Selva and the sanctuary imbued every breath of the jungle, every ripple in the river, and the protective energy surrounding us. The golden chariot, the horses, and the celestial entourage served merely as symbols of his eternal presence—manifestations of the spiritual essence that continued to provide refuge for this sacred place.

The realization dawned on me: Don Howard's essence transcended the limitations of the physical realm. He was intricately connected to this hallowed ground, filled with his spirit, vigilantly overseeing Selva and all those in pursuit of healing and enlightenment. His protection was timeless and omnipresent, a constant energy guiding us. This awareness filled me with reverence and appreciation as I began to understand the profound depth of his connection to the sanctuary, to Selva, and to the divine energy that unites us all.

As I lay in the deep stillness of the maloca, Don Howard's voice surged within me—steady, powerful, and purposeful. He entrusted me with a sacred task, a message that transcended time and space. Gently, he directed my attention to the gold chain and pendant I wore, intricately etched with the symbol of AUM (OM). This symbol was not merely an ornament; it was a profound representation of consciousness itself—a constant reminder of the inseparable unity between the individual soul and the infinite. The "A" stands for the waking state, the realm in which we engage with the physical world and form the foundation of our experiences. The "U" symbolizes the dream state, a space of endless potential where the subconscious weaves lessons and aligns more closely with our essence. The "M" represents deep sleep, the dormant stillness that holds our unexpressed potential. Beyond these layers, the crescent and dot represent *Maya* —the illusion that clouds ultimate reality—and *Turiya,* the pure, boundless awareness that transcends all forms. Together, these elements encapsulate the journey of the soul, from the illusion of separation to the liberation of oneness.

Wrapped around the pendant, inscribed in delicate script, were the words " *Morte Prima di Disonore* ." Don Howard explained that this inscription denotes the banner under which all warriors fight. It represents a sacred calling: a duty to carry forth honor and truth on the spiritual path. These words became the standard for those who, like me, were walking the path of awakening—a reminder that the fight was not just external but deeply internal, to conquer the illusions of the self and align with the divine purpose.

What struck me most was how I had been guided to commission this pendant. After my second retreat at Nimea Kaya, I returned home with an inexplicable urge to have it made. I couldn't explain why or how, but the pull was undeniable. The pendant was not something I consciously chose; it was as if a deeper part of me knew it was necessary for the next step of my journey. The symbols, the inscription, and the chain came together in a way that resonated with the sacred assignment for which I was unknowingly being prepared.

Through Mother Ayahuasca's revelation, I came to understand that the pendant I wore was not mine to keep but rather a sacred instrument entrusted to me for Selva. Don Howard commissioned it for a profound purpose: to serve as her guardian during the upcoming Ayahuasca ceremonies. This pendant was meant to anchor Selva firmly in the essence of her being while allowing her to navigate the expansive, timeless realms of Turiya. As the clarity about its significance dawned on me, I realized that the design itself had been orchestrated through Mother Ayahuasca's guidance, with my role being to bring it into existence.

The pendant was not simply an adornment but a vessel of profound energy. Each symbol etched into its surface resonated with deep layers of consciousness, vibrating at a frequency aligned with the wisdom spread throughout the universe. The pendant was not intended for me; it was a symbol meant for Selva to illuminate her path and safeguard her. The gravity of this insight instilled in me a profound reverence for the responsibility I carried—a sacred commitment to safeguarding her well-being and spiritual enlightenment.

The significance of this revelation settled within me, evoking a profound sense of trust and duty. Don Howard's message didn't end there; with reverence reverberating in the air, he disclosed a profound truth that filled me with wonder. He spoke of Selva and her approaching journey. Soon, she would give birth to a son, a child destined not just for any life but as the reincarnation of Don Howard himself. He chose to incarnate to ensure Selva would learn to love him as her child, mirroring the love he held for her. The child was to be conceived via the genetic material drawn from me during the ceremony. This notion, initially unsettling and shrouded in mystery, now felt like a divinely orchestrated piece of a grander design.

As he spoke, the weight of his words permeated my being. The child would carry forward Don Howard's spirit and legacy, entwined with Selva in a love as profound and timeless as the Amazon rainforest itself. This revelation was humbling, revealing the intricate tapestry of events—the extraction of genetic material and the role I was destined to fulfill within this sacred unfolding. I sensed the love and purpose weaving through these words—a love that spanned lifetimes, connecting us in a cosmic dance of destiny.

I understand that this was not merely a physical birth; it was the emergence of something far grander—a continuation of a legacy that transcends time, space, and form. The child would embody the wisdom of the ancestors, divine power, and an eternal bond to the earth. The ceremony served not only as a purification of the body but also as a spiritual renewal, preparing us for this momentous occasion. As Don Howard's presence faded, I remained in quiet contemplation, absorbing the gravity of the task entrusted to me, aware that my role in this sacred journey was unfolding.

A question lingered in my heart: I asked Mother Ayahuasca whether my Indian brother, who lay nearby, had attained enlightenment. Her response was laced with teasing warmth: "Do you think someone like you would have an unenlightened guru?" The humor in her tone sparked laughter within me, prompting me to stifle my mirth, cautious not to disrupt the tranquility of the maloca. When I ventured to ask whether I had achieved enlightenment, she responded with playful exasperation, "You are Shiva. What higher truth could there be?" This realization struck me with clarity, and an uncontrollable joy surged within me, erupting into laughter—an expression of divine insight and cosmic humor, a bliss that connected me to the profound and ineffable truth of existence.

As dawn broke the morning after the ceremony, it illuminated the jungle canopy with soft, golden rays. The floral bath awaiting us was unlike any I had encountered. Two shamans, a husband-and-wife team who guided us through the night, set the sacred space. Nestled among towering trees, the area was filled with the rich aromas of damp earth and blooming flowers mingling with the blessed air. The cool, aromatic water they crafted bore petals and sacred herbs prepared with love and intention. As they poured it over me, a profound chill raced down my skin, and each drop cleansed my soul.

Their presence was grounding, and the sacred icaros they sang created an invisible balm of healing that enveloped the air. The melodies coursed through me like a river of light, lifting the burdens of the previous days—my struggles, fears, and doubts dissipated. Each note ushered in a deep release as the remnants of darkness melted away into nothingness. With each moment, I felt lighter, as if the heaviness I once carried had been washed away, leaving only pure, unblemished peace behind.

In that stillness, my most profound transformation unfolded. As the last remnants of water cascaded over me, I experienced something extraordinary: all was gone—the burdens, uncertainties, and worries that had clouded my thoughts, along with the attachments that had held me, were washed away. I sensed the essence of Lord Shiva within me—not as something external, but as the very soul of my being. No longer separated from the Absolute, I was not simply connected to Shiva; I was Shiva. This truth flooded me with an overwhelming sense of wholeness and divine union, revealing that I had always housed this energy, even though I hadn't recognized it.

In the aftermath, the surroundings transformed. The jungle, the sky, and the air—all shimmered with unparalleled clarity as if the entire universe inhaled and exhaled, and I was part of that breath. No longer did I seek answers. I understood that I encompassed everything, and everything resided within me. The ceremony purified not only my body but also my soul, unveiling the eternal truth: I am Shiva—timeless, limitless, and accessible.

Later that day, while reflecting on the night's profound events, I approached the Star Deck to speak with Selva. A flutter of nervous energy danced in my chest as I neared her, the pendant cradled in my hands. As I began to recount my visions, her piercing gaze locked onto mine as if she were delving into the depths of my soul. Her gaze penetrated beyond ordinary observation; it stripped away all facades, revealing realities that I had not yet comprehended. Vulnerability swept through me, leaving me utterly exposed yet surprisingly comfortable.

I presented her with the pendant, my voice quaking slightly as I relayed the visions. Selva accepted it with grace, her spirit radiating a silent, knowing acceptance that electrified the moment with profound peace and connection. In her hands, the pendant felt preordained.

As we approached the maloca, we contemplated the events of the previous night. Selva confirmed my unsettling experience: the haunting, otherworldly sounds echoing through the maloca were clear signs of a powerful, malevolent entity. She explained that addressing this presence required the collective effort of all four shamans. The seriousness of her message resonated with me, revealing an irrefutable reality. I remembered the other participants I had met earlier, each visibly disturbed by the sounds they had experienced and expressed their fear as they tried to make sense of it. They had not simply heard noises; they had sensed a dark energy reaching into their beings. I smiled, recalling that I was at the heart of it all, creating a safe space and enveloping everyone in love while protecting Selva and the sanctuary from incomprehensible threats.

This understanding wrapped around me—not as a weight, but as a profound responsibility. Selva's quiet affirmation, the way she gazed into my soul and recognized truths I hadn't voiced, deepened my conviction. I had come here for a purpose—to stand as a guardian in the presence of darkness, to protect and serve Shakti, the light within Selva. The clarity of this intention filled me with both wonder and humility, and as we parted ways, I felt more aligned with the sacred journey than ever before.

Chapter Eleven

The Gift of Unconditional Love

The second ceremony commenced in the familiar warmth and sacred atmosphere of the maloca. A charged stillness enveloped the room as each participant awaited their turn to drink the medicine. Outside, the jungle hummed with vibrant sounds, while inside the maloca, an unvoiced consensus thrummed—something amazing awaited us. As I drank from my full cup, the potent, bitter taste lingered in my mouth, signaling the journey that lay ahead. I settled onto my mat, ready to surrender to the experience and trusting the medicine to guide me.

Minutes elongated into what felt like hours. The atmosphere thickened around me; despite my acute awareness and racing heart, visions eluded me. There was no sign of Mother Ayahuasca's presence, only the gentle resonance of the maloca surrounding me. I remained patient, each second drawing me closer to the connection I yearned for. My thoughts spiraled, craving the guidance I had received so powerfully in past ceremonies. Amid the silence, I discerned a profound truth: sometimes, the ceremony demands patience, and tonight, perhaps, it was meant simply to wait.

The room fell quiet for a brief moment. As time trickled by, my brothers and sisters began to yield to the medicine's influence. The first sounds of retching reverberated through the maloca, accompanied by a chorus of groans and sobs. The anguished cries echoed against the wooden walls, crafting a jarring blend of liberation, openness, and grief. Their suffering settled heavily in the air, an emotional fog that tugged at my heart. Although their distress felt overwhelming, I understood that this was an integral part of the ceremony, a necessary aspect of the purging process. The intense sounds, while disconcerting, were essential to the transformation unfolding around us.

I recalled my purpose for being there: I had come to serve others, to hold space for their pain. Taking a steadying breath, I closed my eyes, imagining love radiating throughout the room. I visualized waves of compassion emanating from my heart, enveloping each soul present in the maloca. My energy became a warm embrace, surrounding those around me with a healing glow. This was not merely an act of empathy; it was a profound, unspoken bond, a reminder that we were united in this sacred, transformative space.

To my left, a young woman's voice pierced through the chorus of distress, trembling as she called out for Selva, the revered caretaker of the sanctuary. Her words, frail and steeped in fear, sought comfort amid her purging. Almost instantaneously, Selva appeared, a gentle light illuminating the darkness.

Her presence exuded warmth and compassion, epitomizing divine maternal grace. With quiet resolve, Selva knelt beside the young woman, her arms open in a gesture of unconditional love. The entire maloca stood still, collectively experiencing the gravity of this sacred exchange.

As Selva enveloped her in an embrace, a profound tenderness suffused the air. This was more than a physical connection; Selva cradled the woman's spirit, extending not only her presence but also her very essence. The touch was gentle yet charged with significant healing energy that flowed directly from her heart. She spoke softly to the woman, her voice a soothing balm that eased her internal turmoil. There was no rush, no urgency. Selva's care was thorough and patient, as if time itself had decelerated to honor this moment of deep healing.

Tears brimmed in my eyes as I observed this scene. I was witnessing the Divine Mother herself tending to her child, offering solace and strength. The purity of Selva's love transcended human limitations; it was a love that sought nothing in return, existing solely to give and heal. An overwhelming sense of gratitude surged within me. I had been granted a rare glimpse of something sacred and eternal. The connection between Selva and the soul in her care was far beyond mere physicality; it was a spiritual exchange that imbued the maloca with an indescribable reverence.

In that tranquil moment, I was reminded of love's remarkable healing power. Selva's dedication and complete presence fostered a wave of wonder and respect. It was a testament to the boundless, unconditional love that exists throughout the universe—a love that transcends time, space, and even comprehension. This experience humbled me, revealing the sacredness of awakening not just within the maloca but also within the hearts of all those seeking healing.

As the participants slowly regained their composure and their purging experiences subsided, the atmosphere in the maloca shifted. The tension began to ease, making way for a growing sense of tranquility. The earlier tumult of voices receded, leaving only the soft whispers of the jungle to fill the newly embraced quiet. In this suspended silence, Mother Ayahuasca revealed her presence, her spirit filling the space. Her voice, both soothing and authoritative, enveloped me in a warmth that reached the very depths of my being.

"Isn't it more fulfilling to share your love without waiting for their request?" she inquired, her words slicing through the silence like a gentle breeze. Her tone was playful, nudging me toward a deeper understanding of love's nature. There was no reproach, only an invitation to grasp a more profound truth about unconditional love. Her wisdom resonated deeply and was meant for everyone present. It served as a reminder that love shouldn't be conditional or wait for acknowledgment. Instead, it should flow freely, like an uninterrupted stream that does not seek permission to be shared.

Mother Ayahuasca referenced an earlier moment from the day, a lighthearted exchange I had enjoyed with the group. I had jokingly described unconditional love, hoping to inject humor, though, in my heart, I recognized the truth behind my words. "If anyone were to open me up, they would find only unconditional love," I had said, chuckling at the thought. It was a light comment intended to lift the mood, but in the presence of the medicine, it took on profound significance.

She chuckled softly, her tone warm and inviting. "You weren't serious, were you? Asking someone to open you up would be quite a mess, and we certainly don't want that," she teased playfully, her soft laughter reverberating in my mind. I couldn't help but smile; the lightness of her remarks lifted my spirits while hinting at deeper insights hidden within her humor. Her voice served as a reminder that joy can coexist with profound wisdom.

As the laughter faded, her tone shifted to one of gentle seriousness, carrying substantial weight. "Simply share your unconditional love," she instructed, her message clear and unambiguous. It was a simple declaration, yet its depth echoed within me like a resonant chord striking my heart. I understood that love requires no permission; it doesn't need to be earned or quantified. Genuine love is given freely, without expectation or conditions. It's not about waiting for others to ask; it's about offering love inherently because that is the essence of love itself.

Her words settled in my heart like seeds planted in rich soil, poised to blossom into something profound. The concept of unconditional love, which I had previously understood intellectually, began to intertwine with my being. I could feel its presence growing within me, roots extending through my awareness. This was a love that demanded no reciprocation, a love that didn't seek gain. It was pure and boundless, ready to be shared with the world.

The more I pondered her guidance, the clearer it became that this wasn't solely about loving others; it encompassed loving myself in the same way. Unconditional love wasn't confined to my interactions with others; it involved embracing myself entirely and accepting every facet of my being without judgment. The wisdom of her words ignited something within me, unlocking a sense of freedom marked by a willingness to love without limitations, hesitation, or fear.

Mother Ayahuasca's voice resonated with calmness and nurturing warmth as she acknowledged the physical discomfort that weighed heavily upon me. She knew the exhaustion that had settled in my body due to fasting, as well as the unsettling churn in my stomach. "I know your struggle," she spoke in a gentle, soothing tone reminiscent of a caregiver reassuring their ward. Her words were like a soft embrace, offering relief as she recognized my trials without demanding more than I could bear.

Her empathy acted as a balm, a reminder that this path was not solely about confronting my shadows but also about honoring my humanity. She perceived me not just as a spiritual seeker in pursuit of enlightenment but also as a weary human in need of compassion and care. "I won't make you purge," she reassured me, her voice comforting and understanding. "Your body doesn't need that now." This recognition of my limitations grounded me, reinforcing the idea that Mother Ayahuasca's wisdom centered on guiding us through healing rather than pushing us to our limits.

In her presence, I felt an overwhelming sense of security—an assurance that I was supported in my challenges. There was no urgency to excel or to push through discomfort. Instead, she advocated for gentleness, granting me the space to simply be, to rest, and to exist without the burden of action. "Just take a break and relax," she encouraged softly. Her invitation felt like a tender nudge to surrender, allowing me to pause, breathe, and trust that this ceremony would unfold at its own pace.

I obeyed her guidance, lying back on the mat and allowing my body to sink into the earth beneath me. A wave of relief swept over me as I closed my eyes, welcoming the stillness. There was no compulsion to push; I could simply rest, recognizing that this tranquil moment was as sacred as the intense experiences I had. I felt my body loosen and my thoughts quiet, and I embraced the opportunity to relax fully, confident in the divine care that surrounded me.

I stood motionless, contemplating the valuable lessons and experiences I had accumulated. My curiosity, though momentarily subdued, continued to flicker beneath the surface. As if attuned to my silent desire for greater insights, Mother Ayahuasca's voice broke the stillness. "What else do you want?" she asked, her tone light and playful.

I took a moment, the weight of her question pressing against my mind. Finally, I whispered, "To teach me." My words flowed with a softness that masked the profound yearning for wisdom within me. I felt a twinge of vulnerability in asking, uncertain of what response awaited me. Mother Ayahuasca's answer came swiftly, her voice infused with playful curiosity: "Teach you what?" The simplicity of her inquiry caught me off guard, prompting a deeper reflection on the vastness of the knowledge still before me.

I inhaled deeply, organizing my thoughts before speaking again. "What I don't know," I replied, feeling exposed in this moment of honesty. The realization of my ignorance loomed large, stirring a mix of wonder and humility within me. Her laughter, warm and affectionate, filled the air, easing the edges of my uncertainty. It embraced my spirit, a gentle reminder that there was only love.

"There is so much you don't know," she responded, her voice tender yet infused with profound wisdom. "But we don't have time for that now." I felt the truth of her words settle within me, prompting a shift toward being present rather than getting lost in an ocean of questions. "Stay with what you know; that's good enough," she advised her words resonating with clarity. This reminded me to anchor myself in the wisdom I had already accumulated, trusting that it was sufficient while making space for deeper understandings to unfold in their rightful time.

Before fading, Mother Ayahuasca offered one final question: "Do you want to see anything else?" Her tone was casual, but her words carried a deeper meaning. She hinted that, having peeled away all the layers of illusion and unveiled Shiva's energy within me, anything else I might experience would now appear like a movie—an illusion played out on a screen, knowing it was not real. The weight of her insight settled into my heart, and I smiled, feeling profound serenity fill the space. "No, thank you," I replied, my voice calm and content. I understood then that the answers I had been searching for were not to be found in more visions or experiences but in the stillness within—the resolute truth of the self beyond all illusions.

I sank into the embrace of the maloca, feeling its vibrant energy surround me. The sanctuary resembled the heart of a divine landscape, an eternal refuge where the sacred and the pristine seamlessly converge. It was an experience of profound wholeness, as if I had merged with something eternal and unchanging.

In that tranquility, I sensed Selva's spiritual guardianship radiating throughout the maloca like an invisible yet powerful force. Though not physically visible, her presence was unmistakable—a luminous beacon of divine light woven into the fabric of this sacred space. She had merged with the energy of the maloca, serving as a holder of the sacred work unfolding. I felt her protection and love, as well as her connection to the Divine, grounding me more firmly in the present.

With each deep breath, I sank further into a profound sense of peace and belonging. The jungle outside had quieted; the gentle concerto of life was now a distant murmur. In that sacred silence, I understood that I no longer needed to seek answers. I was precisely where I ought to be: cradled, sheltered, and connected to the infinite energy around me. The journey wasn't over, yet I felt complete.

When the ceremony reached its conclusion, I made a choice that, in hindsight, proved ill-advised. Instead of remaining in the comforting cocoon of the maloca, I decided to return to my room, hoping for rest and respite. The notion of lying down in the stillness of my space felt instinctive, but as soon as I settled, my surroundings began to shift. Disorientation set in, accompanied by a wave of nausea as if the air itself had turned hostile. Mother

Ayahuasca's voice, soft yet incisive, echoed in my mind, carrying both playful warmth and resolute clarity. "Are you prepared to throw up?" she asked, her voice laced with a knowing edge.

Taken aback by her question, I reminded her of our previous understanding. "I thought we had an agreement," I replied, attempting to rationalize my choice. Her response was measured, tinged with amusement yet underscored by seriousness: "Yes, but you were supposed to remain in the maloca until dawn." The impact of her words struck me instantly. I had breached a sacred guideline intended to protect and keep me anchored within the spiritual energy of the ceremony. In my folly, I had disregarded her guidance and ventured out alone, believing I could withstand the experience independently.

With a blend of hesitance and resolve, I made my way back to the maloca. Each step felt laborious as if I were climbing a steep hill, my body weighed down by both physical strain and a sense of spiritual disarray. The moist jungle served as a tangible reminder of my deviation from the sacred place. The trees loomed around me, their shadows swaying like specters, reflecting my inner conflict. The forest seemed to stand vigil, its presence heavy with judgment as I chose to step away from the sanctity of the maloca.

As I retraced my steps, I scolded myself for ignoring the insights I had received. The maloca served as my refuge. Within its hallowed confines, the energies of the ceremony could continue their delicate weaving, and by stepping outside, I had unwittingly disrupted a process beyond my comprehension. In my eagerness to flee discomfort,

I had severed a bond of spiritual safeguarding, leaving me to confront the fallout. The profundity of this realization rendered each step increasingly significant, pulling me back to where I truly belonged to reconnect with the spiritual sanctuary awaiting me in the maloca.

In front of me stood the maloca, a bastion of the spirit, its wooden structure alive with the echoes of countless prayers and chants. Every plank exuded the energy of past rituals, its foundation a deep well of shared intention and divine protection. I could feel this life force surging; the maloca was more than mere timber—it was a vibrant being, ready to embrace me once again.

As I approached the maloca, a powerful energy wrapped around my being like a protective shield, offering refuge from the turmoil I had just left behind. The air became filled with energy, gentle yet commanding, drawing me in with a quiet authority. The maloca seemed to call to me, reminding me of the sanctuary I had momentarily departed. My heartbeat slowed, and the space invited me to release my anxieties and simply be. With each step closer to the entrance, my breath steadied, and my pulse returned to a calm rhythm as if the atmosphere were guiding me toward tranquility.

Upon entering the sacred space of the maloca, I immediately felt a profound sense of belonging. The shift in energy was both immediate and profound, as though the maloca absorbed my unease and replaced it with serenity. The tension that had been coiling in my body melted away completely, leaving only a sense of stillness. The disorienting sensations that had plagued me moments earlier disappeared as if the maloca's very essence had the power to recalibrate my being, restoring harmony and balance to every part of me.

I had returned to a sacred space that knew my essence at a profound depth. Surrounding me was a charged atmosphere, healing energy that wrapped me tightly, allowing me to breathe freely and be wholly present without the burdens of the past. The maloca, steeped in sacred chants and prayers, provided the grounding I had unconsciously yearned for.

I sank into my mat, my body still vibrating with the residual currents of the ceremony. The overwhelming relief and gratitude felt innocent and unguarded, as if I had returned to the embrace of a nurturing parent. Every muscle released its tension, surrendering wholeheartedly to the sanctuary I had just re-entered. I silently expressed my thanks to Mother Ayahuasca for her gentle reminder, humbled by the teachings rooted in the sacred paths that had led me here. The maloca felt like a shrine, a home for my soul amidst the vastness of existence.

It was a living entity, a sanctuary offering protection and profound healing. More than just a ceremonial site, it embodied spiritual resilience. A thousand prayers of renewal and grounding echoed within, calling me back to my center. The air thrummed with energy, revealing that this was not a mere structure; it was a divine refuge, sacred and substantial.

Mother Ayahuasca's voice resonated once more in my thoughts, emphasizing the sanctity of the maloca. "This is Shiva's abode," she proclaimed reverently. A shiver traveled through me as her words took root, imparting the immense significance of this place. She had guided me to this point to affirm that I stood within the most sacred site in the Americas. This particular maloca wasn't merely wood and thatch; it was a divine temple imbued with Shiva's energy, a realm where healing and transformation flourished. Her insights filled me with awe, forging an unbreakable bond with the ancient spirit of this land.

I shut my eyes to fully embrace the essence of the maloca. The atmosphere felt rejuvenating, nourishing my soul. The sweet aroma of floral offerings blended with the rich scent of sacred tobacco and smoldering sage, crafting an environment that was both anchoring and freeing. Outside, the jungle thrummed with its ancient cadence: the chirping of crickets, the whispering of leaves, and the sporadic calls of nocturnal animals resonated in the background. The soundscape of the jungle harmonized with the sanctity of the space, creating a tranquil symphony of existence that felt both eternal and boundless. I understood the profound wisdom of staying here, aware that it provided a unique sense of divine protection and healing. Mother Ayahuasca's guidance and the energy of the sanctuary would illuminate the road ahead on my journey.

My heart brimmed with gratitude, not only for my liberation from discomfort but also for the wisdom nestled within the experience. I had been reminded, once again, of the necessity of honoring sacred rituals and trusting the spiritual guardians guiding my path. Rejuvenated, I reminded myself to cultivate mindfulness, embracing the ceremony's teachings with honor and respect. As the gentle energy of the maloca surrounded me, I found solace in the truth that I was precisely where I needed to be: safe, supported, and immensely thankful.

The next day, the shamans gathered us again for a sacred floral bath. The early morning air remained cool, infused with the aromatic essence of flowers and herbs steeped in moonlit water overnight. One by one, we approached the curandero and curandera, who stood with serene authority, their hands both gentle and intentional as they practiced their art. As they poured the fragrant water over me, a wave of serenity flowed down my body, cleansing not only the physical remnants of the previous night's journey but also the lingering emotional and spiritual heaviness.

The floral bath felt like a rebirth, with the water—infused with petals and healing herbs—caressing my skin and promising renewal. The cool droplets cascaded down my face and shoulders, each touch lifting away residual energies from the ceremony, clarifying my mind and calming my spirit. I stood there with folded hands, welcoming the embrace of the floral waters. An overwhelming sense of gratitude surged through me, my heart swelling with the profound lessons of unconditional love and spiritual humility imparted by the ceremony. Mother Ayahuasca's whispers softly echoed within me, preparing me to greet a new day with reverence for the experience and the intention to live mindfully.

Around me, my spiritual brothers and sisters underwent similar transformations. Faces that had appeared drawn and pale the night before now radiated with vitality, and spirits once burdened by emotional release danced lightly. The group exuded a collective energy of renewal, with an unspoken bond of healing threading us together. We exchanged smiles, some even laughing gently, relieved to have shared the night's trials.

Joy filled the air, an unvoiced acknowledgment of the struggles we had faced and the wisdom we had gained. A quiet celebration embraced us, with conversations flowing naturally as each person eagerly and lightly shared their experiences. The atmosphere thrummed with animated chatter, yet the cadence remained gentle, as if time itself had slowed, allowing us to fully absorb and appreciate the lessons we had learned. There was no rush, only peaceful camaraderie—a shared understanding that we had journeyed through profound transformation together.

Seated with my brothers and sisters as they enjoyed their breakfast, I observed the vibrancy of the outside world, which mirrored the uplifting energy within. The jungle around us throbbed with life, and the sounds of the wildlife blended harmoniously with the warmth radiating from our hearts. Birds chirped in a jubilant chorus while the sunlight, vibrant and full, filtered through the lush canopy, casting golden patterns on the forest floor. The sunrays danced with the gentle breeze, creating a rhythm that echoed the renewed pulse of our spirits. The act of sharing space and conversation, despite our fasting, filled me with a deep sense of community and unity. The entire Amazon seemed to rejoice alongside us, welcoming us back into the natural cycle of life with open arms.

United in quiet connection, we basked in the embrace of the morning sun and the sweet aroma of nature, infused with a soft hum of contentment. The sacredness of our shared experience lingered, not as grand revelations but in a profound peace and connection to all that surrounded us. No longer merely individuals, we amalgamated into a community of souls—brothers and sisters—bound by the deep understanding of our shared journey.

An unspoken commitment united us: that the insights gained during the ceremony would persist, woven into the tapestry of our lives. The healing had merely begun, and we would now step forward, each carrying a fragment of that sacred experience within, prepared to confront the world with newfound clarity.

Chapter Twelve

The Healing Waters of Forgiveness

In the third ceremony, Mother Ayahuasca continued to weave her transformative energy, crafting an ambiance of serenity and profound healing. After drinking only half a cup, I felt a soothing tranquility enhanced by the collective energy in the maloca, which had softened compared to earlier ceremonies. The fragrant blend of herbal aromas mingled with the incense gently wafting throughout the maloca, creating a sacred atmosphere that was both grounding and uplifting. Every inhalation was imbued with the Earth's ancient wisdom as if the air had absorbed the timeless essence of the rainforest. It served as a reminder that, despite being a man-made structure, the maloca was intricately linked to the life energy of the jungle—a profound connection that surpassed the limits of time and space. The shamans' icaros, powerful and archaic, saturated the room with energy, weaving an invisible net of protection that enveloped us. The melodic chants surrounded us like a cocoon, fostering an unspoken bond that allowed each participant to feel both singular and united on this spiritual journey.

The rhythm of the ceremony resonated so perfectly with the natural world that it seemed as if the entire structure were inhaling and exhaling alongside the trees and nocturnal animals beyond the walls. The jungle outside, teeming with life and sound, felt like an extension of the maloca, as if both entities were parts of a singular living organism. In this shared breath of existence, time lost its conventional grip; the space felt boundless, stretching far beyond the realm of the physical.

As I surrendered to the environment, I felt that the energy in the maloca had shifted from the intensity of the earlier rituals. It felt gentler and more serene as if a deeper layer of healing had begun. My fellow spiritual seekers radiated tranquility, their expressions reflecting a peace that had eluded many of them in the preceding nights. There was grace in their movements, a lightness pervading their presence. It seemed as though the collective energy had achieved a newfound balance—one where healing was beginning to take root within each individual. The atmosphere conveyed a sense of acceptance: of one another, of the process unfolding, and of the transformative essence of the Ayahuasca itself.

I sat silently on my mat, feeling the comforting warmth of the Earth sustaining me and anchoring me in the moment. The maloca exuded a sense of divinity, its energy palpably vibrant. Though the half cup of Ayahuasca hadn't yet unveiled visions, the serene stillness I embraced was not disconcerting. Instead, it opened me to the present, sharpening my awareness of the energy surrounding me.

I directed my focus outward, sending love and healing to each person in the space. With my eyes closed, I envisioned golden waves of light cascading from my heart, enveloping everyone in radiant warmth and compassion. This exchange required no elaborate words or gestures; it was a simple act of energy, a gift of love offered without expectation. The more I concentrated on this image, the more I felt the warmth expanding, not just to those near me but throughout the maloca, filling the room with a nearly tangible serenity.

As I immersed myself in this act of sharing, the once-charged atmosphere began to soften. The harmonious hum of the jungle blended with the united energy of all participants, gradually crafting a more balanced ambiance. My gesture of love seemed to create a ripple effect, affecting others in ways that were beyond visibility but deeply felt. The room, which had previously pulsed with restlessness, now felt like a sacred haven—a space for collective healing and shared purpose.

The palpable sense of relief in the space manifested as a collective sigh of release, signaling that we had all unburdened ourselves from the tension that had accumulated during the ceremonies. People were no longer in a state of struggle or anticipation. Instead, they exuded a quiet comfort in their postures and breaths, allowing themselves to simply exist. I felt a profound peace within, understanding that my serene act of devotion contributed to the overarching harmony of the maloca. The collective connection among everyone present had never felt so tangible.

An hour and a half into the ceremony, I lay on my back, gazing up at the intricately woven dome above and feeling the sacred weight of the space gently pressing down. My body was relaxed, yet my mind remained vigilant, eagerly awaiting the life-altering effects of Ayahuasca. Suddenly, the familiar and nurturing voice of Mother Ayahuasca surrounded me, resonating within like a gentle wave, anchoring and expanding my consciousness.

"You have an unaltered cup and a half of medicine within you," she uttered, her voice reverberating deeply within me. "Therefore, you can speak on my behalf." Her clarity was infused with authority and compassion, and the depth of her presence enveloped me in a protective yet nurturing embrace. This was not merely a message; it was an invitation, a sacred responsibility. I felt her guidance urging me to understand that this was a moment steeped in purpose.

In that eerie stillness, she assigned me a task that would reveal my compassion. "You must talk with the woman who carried the demonic entity," she instructed, her tone both firm and tender. "Extend to her my message of forgiveness and well-being for her bravery in releasing the darkness she has held." I absorbed her words, aware that this endeavor was not solely about my interaction with the woman but about healing on a grander scale. It was an opportunity to deliver the divine message of release and to let go of the burdens we often carry unknowingly.

The gravity of her words settled within me, bringing a profound sense of duty. Although daunting, this task felt like a bridge between the sacred and the secular. I could sense the weight of responsibility, not only as a voice for Mother Ayahuasca but also as a channel for the energy of forgiveness and healing. I was meant to offer something far more significant than mere words; I was to convey a spiritual truth that could guide her toward liberation, releasing the malevolent energy she had held. The clarity of my role endowed me with calm determination, and I realized I was being steered not only by Mother Ayahuasca but also by the sacred space we had co-created within the maloca.

A surge of warmth and love coursed through me as I listened to Mother Ayahuasca's guidance, her words echoing within my heart. The energy in the maloca pulsed rhythmically, aligning with the heartbeat of the Earth. Every element in the space—every inhalation, flicker of candlelight, and rustle of the jungle—existed in synchrony, nurturing and supporting the sacred work in which we were engaged. A profound gratitude welled up within me, not just for the experience but also for the maloca itself, which had transformed into a vessel of healing. I understood that my spiritual brothers and sisters, each on unique quests, were undergoing their profound changes. Regardless of our distinct paths, a palpable sense of unity anchored us all, an invisible thread weaving through the space and binding us in a collective experience of growth and spiritual awakening.

The love enveloping the room felt like an embrace, surrounding me and every soul in the maloca. Healing vibrations rippled through the walls, extending far beyond the physical structure into the heart of the jungle. This reminder of our interconnectedness affirmed that we were parts of a much larger whole—an intricate web of energy and purpose. This realization surged through me, embodying the strength of our collective journey and acknowledging that we were supporting each other in ways that might remain beyond our comprehension. It was a humbling and inspiring moment, a beautifully clear insight into the profound work in which we were involved.

Needing a moment to ground myself amidst it all, I quietly rose from my seat and ventured outside. The jungle welcomed me with its warm embrace as I inhaled deeply, savoring the rich, earthy aroma of the vibrant flora. The lush canopy overhead provided a protective shroud around the sacred maloca, and the distant sounds of the jungle blended harmoniously with the rustling leaves and unseen wildlife, grounding me further. With every breath, I deepened my bond with the Earth, affirming that my presence in that moment was exactly as it should be.

The serene jungle mirrored the stillness settling in my mind. Closing my eyes, I felt the Earth's gentle pressure underfoot, anchoring me in the present. The energy from the maloca, along with the profound teachings of Mother Ayahuasca, flowed through me like a tranquil current. I inhaled deeply, releasing the lingering tension from the ceremony, allowing myself to simply be—knowing that every forward step in this journey would unfold in divine timing. The ancient wisdom and vibrant life force of the jungle echoed this truth: each event has its moment, and everything was as it should be.

Returning to the maloca, I was immediately captivated by the sight of my Indian brother meditating in the center, fully immersed in deep contemplation. His posture was a striking embodiment of stability, his back perfectly aligned and his hands resting gently on his knees. The serenity emanating from him created an aura of sacred stillness that enveloped the space around him. His presence was both magnetic and grounding, and a profound sense of reverence engulfed me for the devotion he had dedicated to his practice. There was a complete absence of urgency in his movements—only a palpable calm resonated throughout the room.

Emboldened by the purity of his spirit, I chose to unite my energy with his. I folded my legs beneath me and settled onto the floor, finding a serene seat that grounded me. As I embraced the stillness, the atmosphere thickened, suffused with a haunting quiet that filled the space. Upon closing my eyes, a deep wave of calm coursed through me, prompting my breath to deepen. The din of the external world drifted away, leaving behind only the soothing rhythm of my inhales and exhales, along with the gentle whisper of leaves swaying in the jungle beyond. The room transformed into a sanctuary for inner stillness—a channel to reconnect with the divine energy that flows within all beings.

Minutes elongated into an infinite experience as I sank further into my meditation. Time lost its significance, ebbing away unnoticed as I harmonized with the surrounding energies. The tranquility I sought wrapped around me like a gentle embrace that felt like a soft, cozy blanket. There was a release of tension and an absence of urgency—only the unbroken flow of breath and existence remained. The maloca and the vibrant jungle outside became a cohesive tapestry, leaving me in synchrony with the unfolding spiritual energy. The enriching silence deepened, crafting a sacred space where stray thoughts and distractions were unwelcome.

In this shared stillness, I sensed an unspoken bond forming with my spiritual brother. We were present in this sacred moment, not as isolated souls but as integral components of a greater unity. The silence between us established a resonance that felt ancient and would blossom within the holy confines of the maloca. I lost track of time while basking in this serenity, allowing the stillness to permeate my being and anchor me in the present. I was not chasing anything; I was simply existing.

Eventually, my Indian brother gracefully rose from his seat and stepped outside with purpose. The serene energy he had fostered lingered in the air, wrapping the space in a tranquil embrace. I inhaled deeply and surrendered myself to relaxation, contemplating the possibility of finally grasping some rest. My body, weary from the intensity of the ceremonies and the emotional labor of previous days, craved rejuvenation. The prospect of yielding to sleep was inviting, so I lay down, allowing my body to meld with the mat below. The soft symphony of the jungle's nighttime sounds blended seamlessly with the silence within the maloca.

Before long, he returned, re-entering the maloca with unwavering calm. He resumed his meditation fluidly, his serene posture undisturbed by his brief departure. His presence permeated the space once again, invigorating it with the luminous energy of his practice. I watched him with a soft smile, feeling a mix of admiration and respect for his discipline. The urge to sleep dissolved, overshadowed by the profound opportunity to join him in this shared spiritual sanctuary.

Drawn by an unseen force, I found myself sitting upright, compelled to reconnect with him. The notion of sleep dissipated, replaced by a deeper calling. I crossed my legs once more and positioned myself to align with the flowing energy surrounding us. Closing my eyes, I surrendered to the enveloping tranquility that now expanded and deepened. The maloca once again transformed into the epicenter of existence, where time lost its grip, and the exchange of spiritual energy became our sole focus.

In our mutual silence, it felt as if we were engaged in an exchange of energies that required no words. Our spiritual connection thrived; our minds and hearts communicated effortlessly, imparting wisdom and support without the need for articulation. The experience was profoundly nourishing—more so than mere rest—akin to two souls drawing from the same well of spiritual energy, sharing unvoiced knowledge and solidifying our bond. As moments elapsed, I realized that this shared meditation held far greater value than any sleep I had anticipated. It became a sacred interaction, enhancing our connection—a gift that I felt honored to receive.

The remainder of the night unfolded peacefully, filled with a gentle stream of healing energy that enveloped the maloca. I sensed the nurturing presence of Mother Ayahuasca as she lovingly worked on our spirits. I felt complete, interconnected, and profoundly grateful for the serene beauty surrounding this ceremony.

The next day beckoned with the anticipation of the floral bath—a ritual resembling a baptism of renewal. The shamans delicately poured cold, fragrant water infused with petals and herbs over me. The liquid cascaded across my skin, cleansing away the remnants of the previous night's ceremony. The aroma of blossoms filled the air, blending with the morning dew, and I experienced a profound sense of renewal—like being reborn into a new day, feeling lighter and infused with hope.

Joy permeated the atmosphere as though the entire sanctuary rejoiced in a hushed celebration. Faces previously marked by exhaustion or emotional strain now radiated newfound brilliance, each person seemingly carrying an inner flame of light. Smiles flowed freely, our expressions warm and gentle, as if an invisible weight had been lifted from our collective shoulders.

Genuine laughter erupted spontaneously, bridging the gap between us, a shared release after enduring profound, transformative experiences. Conversations blossomed with newfound openness, the struggles of the previous night weaving an invisible bond among us, uniting our hearts in a manner that only profound spiritual journeys maintain.

A sense of renewal surged through the sanctuary, permeating everything with brightness and vitality. The jungle mirrored this upliftment—leaves rustled, and birds serenaded us with joyful melodies as if participating in our celebration. The warm sunlight filtered through the trees, enveloping us in a golden aura, rendering the entire space sacred and filled with healing and hope. It was a moment of pure life, where every soul embraced gratitude for existence, feeling interconnected and whole.

I approached the woman Mother Ayahuasca had guided me to connect with, my heart brimming with compassion for her journey. Despite the light that surrounded her, a subtle sadness lingered in her eyes, hinting at her struggles. The shadows that once clung to her had faded, yet the remnants of her past weighed heavily in the depths of her gaze. As I approached, I felt the weighty responsibility of conveying the sacred message entrusted to me, knowing it was integral to her healing process.

With humility, I requested her permission to share what Mother Ayahuasca had imparted to me. Choosing my words with care, I recognized that the truth I carried might be challenging to accept. "Though it may initially seem harsh," I began softly, my voice steady yet compassionate, "it will be washed away in love." I observed her reaction as the words landed; tears welled in her eyes, a mix of sorrow and relief escaping in quiet sobs. With every tear shed, a fragment of the pain she had held for so long was set free, allowing healing to flow in.

The emotional release endured for what felt like an eternity, yet eventually, her sobs subsided. She took a deep breath, and with the final tear, a peaceful smile graced her features. Lightness flooded her spirit as if a long-borne weight had lifted at last. Her once-heavy heart became accessible, her energy now radiating brightness and openness. I felt her gratitude resonate palpably, knowing the message had fulfilled its purpose. The transformation within her was tangible, and I felt honored to have played a part.

The teachings imparted throughout the night left an indelible mark on my soul. The healing was not solely hers; it extended to encompass us all. Each of us was transformed, touched by the sacred energy of the ceremony. Outside, the jungle thrummed with the vibrant sounds of morning. The birds sang jubilantly in the trees, their harmonies filling the air with hope and renewal. Sunlight filtering through the canopy painted the world in golden hues, as if the Earth itself celebrated our collective metamorphosis, rejoicing in the healing and liberation that blossomed within the maloca.

Chapter Thirteen

A Gift of Peace

As the final ceremony approached, I stood on the brink of a profound awakening. Inside the maloca, an atmosphere of shared intention and sacred reverence enshrouded us. One by one, the participants advanced toward the altar, deliberately drinking the thick, murky concoction of Ayahuasca. Their movements radiated a quiet acceptance of the sacred ritual. I witnessed a transformation, sensing a change in my energy with each sip taken. Unexpectedly, a powerful wave of nausea surged through me—intense and inescapable. The sight of the brew, familiar yet alien at that moment, triggered deep discomfort—not merely physical, but a signal from within that something had fundamentally changed.

The nausea escalated, growing from mild unease to a full-bodied reaction. My stomach churned, weighed down by the experience. As I took slow, deep breaths, a realization crystallized in my mind: this moment transcended the brew. It revealed an inner truth—my journey could continue without the medicine. The healing, transformation, and lessons

I sought had already been realized. The ceremonies had meticulously peeled away layers of illusion. The darkness had been expelled, allowing light to take its rightful place within me.

Mother Ayahuasca's presence settled around me with profound clarity; her voice was calm yet firm, conveying a deep knowing: there was no need for more medicine. The truth was simple yet profound—everything I needed had already been imparted. The lessons had woven themselves into the core of my being, leaving no space for further seeking. I stood in quiet acknowledgment of this truth, filled with an overwhelming sense of peace and gratitude. I had attained profound insights from my encounters with Mother Ayahuasca, leaving no further goals to pursue. The journey had naturally concluded, and my responsibility was to honor the gifts I had received, integrating the lessons I had learned and embodying them in my future actions. This was a moment of serene resolution, a recognition that the journey had unfolded as intended.

The ceremony progressed, yet I felt no compulsion to engage in the ritual as I once had. There was an undeniable sense of completion—not only for myself but for everyone gathered in the maloca. I gazed around at my fellow seekers, each on their unique path, and understood that we were interwoven by the invisible threads of healing and change. The collective energy was palpable; the final ceremony represented something greater than the medicine itself—it embodied the profound transformations we had all experienced together. We had arrived at a state of wholeness as one.

My decision to stay sober during this final ceremony arose from a profound realization that I had already attained. I could feel the sacred energy enveloping us and wanted to engage in this last gathering with full awareness. Embracing the silence, I recognized the collective power of the group; each person was attuned to the Divine, and our shared purpose of healing and transformation connected us all.

The shamans began to sing the final icaros, their voices resonating with an energy that transcended the bounds of time. Each note carried the heritage of countless generations—age-old songs that flowed from healer to healer. The icaros felt like threads of divine illumination, weaving the atmosphere into a unified tapestry. The vibrations surged through me, saturating the maloca with a sound that surpassed mere auditory experience; it reached deep into my being, reminding me of the profound importance of the moment.

The maloca itself responded to the icaros; the air was filled with sacred energy. The entire space teemed with life, a sanctuary of utter tranquility. Time dissolved; each moment expanded infinitely, cradling the wisdom of every ceremony that had occurred. Outside, the jungle, which had witnessed so much transformation, receded into the background, contrasting with the profound stillness within.

As the ceremony unfolded, the space remained serene, devoid of purging sounds or cries; it was filled with an all-encompassing sense of peace. The tranquility permeated my entire being, reaching into the deepest places of my soul. I felt genuinely whole as if every fragment of myself had been rekindled and every wound had healed. The maloca, the shamans, the sacred songs, and the ever-watchful jungle combined to create a realm where nothing else was necessary; there was only peace. I felt at home, at ease, and deeply connected to all that had led me here.

Sitting in the quiet of the maloca, a massive presence surrounded me, its energy pulsating like a relentless cosmic force of renewal and dissolution. I felt transported to the essence of Shiva, embodying divine power with each breath and heartbeat. This was not separation but unity with something far greater—an energy that coursed through my entire being. I was fully immersed in the universal cycle of creation and annihilation.

This overwhelming sense of purpose was unlike anything I had ever experienced. It felt as if I were appointed as a silent guardian of this sacred space—a protector of the energy flowing through the maloca. With every inhale, I connected to the heartbeat of existence, an indescribable energy surging through me and intertwining with everything. I was not merely in the maloca; I was the maloca, and everything within and outside it—participants, jungle, and universe—was woven into my consciousness.

While the weight of this responsibility was immense, it felt liberating rather than burdensome. A deep exhilaration coursed through me as if I were tasked with an assignment of immeasurable significance. I was reminded of my role in the cosmic tapestry—an essential part of something vast and ineffable. The realization of my connection to every soul within and outside the maloca—the spirits and energies enveloping us, along with the eternal flow of the universe—filled me with wonder and humility. This was more than a ceremony; it was a moment of cosmic importance.

In the silence of this sacred space, I felt the gravity of this responsibility anchor itself in my heart. It underscored the truth that I was not separate from the universe but instead the source of its fabric. As the ceremony progressed, it became clear that I was here not by happenstance but by purpose—destined to unveil Shiva's energy, and I was prepared to fulfill that calling.

The shamans' icaros engulfed me, their melodies weaving a rich tapestry of healing and spiritual protection. Their songs flowed toward me, the energy surging through sacred melodies, seeking my participation and blessing. My folded hands rested in a state of silent prayer, channeling more than mere reverence. I became a vessel for divine love, radiating immense, compassionate energy outward to all beings present—both inside and outside the maloca. The power flowing through me was both tranquil and formidable, harmonious and complete, as if the universe's compassion had expanded within me.

I saw myself as the guardian of the ceremony, fully engaged in the intent behind each icaros. Each note sung by the shamans wove a canvas of spiritual healing, and as I embodied the energy of Shiva, I transmitted those vibrations into profound healing for everyone present. My heart brimmed with immeasurable, unconditional love, filling the entire atmosphere. It felt as if the cosmos had choreographed this moment of pure tranquility, during which I served as both an observer and a guide—ensuring that every individual around me was shrouded in healing energy.

The next morning, the sanctuary brimmed with vitality, reminiscent of a garden blooming after a refreshing rain. The air vibrated with a palpable sense of renewal as if the jungle itself had assimilated our healing energy and was now resonating with our newly discovered lightness. Each person radiated transformation, moving with effortless grace and an inner luminosity that sparkled in their eyes. Laughter bubbled freely, harmonizing with the whispers of the wind, while even the leaves rejoiced, swaying in rhythm with the gentle breeze.

Conversations flowed with tender joy, imbued with a spirit of shared triumph and profound connection. We exchanged glances rich with understanding; each glance held a fragment of a picture finally complete. The heavyweights we had carried into the ceremonies were lifted, replaced by an unspoken unity that bound us together. The shamans glided among us, their tranquil smiles a reminder of the profound energies that had guided our healing journey. The atmosphere thrummed with celebration and gratitude for the life streaming through us and for the sanctuary that had embraced us in its timeless hold.

The shamans conducted the sacred floral baths, drenching us in the fragrances of revered herbs and blossoms soaked under the moon's gaze. Cold water cascaded over my skin, washing away the remnants of the journey and leaving me feeling revitalized. We shared laughter, our spirits uplifted by the communal metamorphosis. A palpable sense of rebirth surrounded us, with each smile and warm embrace celebrating the collective transformation we had experienced together.

I could feel Mother Ayahuasca's final message resonating deeply within my soul: "To maintain the state of pure consciousness you have achieved, all that is required is to extend unconditional love to everything around you. This love shall be your offering to the world." Her guidance was both straightforward and profoundly resonant, imparting the realization that the ceremonies marked not an ending but the dawn of a new way of existing.

As the huachuma ceremonies approached, a profound clarity emerged. The insight I had long sought became evident, and a deep sense of contentment accompanied this realization. The wisdom of Mother Ayahuasca illuminated my path, transforming my journey from a restless quest into one anchored in confidence. With the essential lessons learned, I felt no compulsion to participate in the upcoming ceremonies; I was happy only to exist in the moment.

The idea of observing the unfolding events as if watching a play brought a comforting tranquility. I understood that ahead lay not a path of endless searching but one of spiritual equilibrium. The lessons imparted had become part of my essence, fully integrated into my being. There was nothing more to seek or acquire; the journey had brought me to a moment of serene empowerment, allowing me to rest, knowing I was whole.

I grasped that the teachings I had received were sufficient. Wisdom and resilience had been bestowed upon me to face whatever lay ahead—not through clinging to more experiences but by embodying what I had already internalized. Mother Ayahuasca's presence revealed that true serenity lies in surrender—in permitting life to unfold without a constant yearning for more. I could embrace the future with trust, prepared for whatever it might offer.

Choosing to withdraw from the ceremonies felt like an act of faith—not a retreat, but a confident acknowledgment that I had gathered all I required. This quiet surrender was an understanding that profound lessons often emerge from stillness and acceptance of the present. With this clarity, I felt anchored and at peace.

An insistent yet gentle pull tugged at my heart, signaling that it was time to depart. Half elated by the gifts I had received and half wistful about leaving this sacred space behind, I began packing. The sanctuary, nestled deep within the Amazon's embrace, was unparalleled in its beauty. Majestic emerald trees danced in the wind while the river glimmered like a silver serpent, weaving through the vivid landscape. The air was rich with the scents of life—moistened earth, fragrant blossoms, and the continuous whisper of the jungle, alive with unseen wonders; the land thrummed with ancient magic.

Descending the steps carved into the riverbank, I was enveloped by the raw, untamed splendor of the Amazon rainforest. The richly saturated greens shimmered vibrantly, with sunlight filtering through the thick canopy to create golden mosaics below. Before me stretched the Amazon River, its waters flowing purposefully, carrying the secrets of the jungle.

The small boat awaiting me bobbed gently in the river's embrace, its wooden form swaying in rhythm with the eternal pulse of the Amazon. A bittersweet mix of emotions filled my heart—profound gratitude for the healing and unfolding of my true nature that I had experienced, yet a sense of sorrow at leaving behind this sacred sanctuary that had nurtured my spirit. I paused and turned to look back, taking in the sight of my spiritual brothers and sisters—each one now woven into the fabric of my soul's journey. We had shared our deepest fears, sorrows, and joys, and through that raw vulnerability, an unbreakable bond had formed among us. I was accompanied by my Indian brother, who had been my guide and from whom I had learned many valuable lessons. I had come to this sanctuary with him, and now, I was leaving with him. It was as though our connection transcended this lifetime, and our shared journey had come full circle.

My brothers and sisters stood resolutely atop the riverbank, waving and beaming, their faces aglow with newfound light. My throat constricted, and emotions swelled as I called out, "I love you. I love you all!" The words flowed from the depths of my heart, resonating through the vibrant jungle. It felt as if the trees and river themselves echoed my farewell—a final blessing destined to linger within this sacred space long after my departure.

As the boat drifted away from the shore, I leaned back, watching the sanctuary gradually fade into the verdant wilderness. The river's gentle current lulled me into contemplation. I realized that while my physical body was leaving, the teachings of Mother Ayahuasca, the spirit of the jungle, and the profound love I had experienced were firmly etched in my heart. The essence of the Amazon, the wisdom of the ceremonies, and the divine presence

I had encountered would accompany me as I reentered the world—whole, transformed, and infused with a renewed sense of purpose.

Epilogue

The journey through the sacred realms of Mother Ayahuasca has proven to be profoundly transformative. What began as a personal pursuit of healing and a search for answers evolved into an experience of immense depth. Each sip of the medicine revealed layers of my essence, uncovering hidden truths long veiled in shadows. Concepts that once felt abstract gradually coalesced into vivid realities, with each ceremony unveiling a fresh chapter in a story that transcends time, allowing me to witness the interconnectedness that binds all existence.

This journey of awakening was not solely about gaining clarity; it was about embodying that clarity in each moment. Insights emerged steadily, akin to pieces of a mosaic aligning with perfect precision. Occasionally, revelations struck like a storm of enlightenment, leaving me breathless in their wake. More frequently, they caressed my consciousness gently, reminiscent of whispers carrying ancient wisdom. The more I surrendered, the more I perceived the world anew through eyes that recognized unity rather than separation.

The narrative I present in this book is not merely an account of visions or mystical experiences. It is a vibrant truth resonating within the universal essence. Every image, emotion, and lesson gleaned from those sacred ceremonies has integrated into my being. These are not fleeting memories; rather, they are present truths awaiting acknowledgment and comprehension. It felt as though Mother Ayahuasca held a mirror before me, reflecting the timeless wisdom that is always accessible yet obscured by the complexities of the mind.

These truths do not need to be discovered; they require us to remember. What we truly desire is always within reach, just beneath our conscious minds. Each ritual acted as a soothing reminder that the solutions I sought were not found outside myself but ingrained deeply within, ready to emerge when the time was right. My awareness always contained this insight, waiting for my recognition. What once felt elusive began to take shape: the timeless wisdom had always been a part of me, patiently awaiting acknowledgment.

Nestled within the vibrant expanse of the Amazon rainforest, I felt a deep connection to the essence of nature. The towering trees shared their wisdom through the fluttering of their leaves, resembling a timeless language, while the air buzzed with the presence of hidden wildlife, creating a lively orchestra that mirrored the river's ceaseless rhythm. Surrounded by verdant life, the environment pulsed with undeniable energy, hinting at deeper truths lying just beneath the surface.

In that sacred environment, the spirit of Mother Ayahuasca surrounded me, her energy embracing me like a nurturing cocoon. She embodied the infinite love, compassion, and wisdom of the Divine Mother. It was not merely a sensation; it was a complete immersion in reverence and openness. Her gentle yet powerful guidance opened my heart and mind, leading me through paths of awareness that had previously gone unconsidered. These revelations transcended abstract notions; they were profoundly personal, almost instinctual insights that connected me to the Ultimate Reality.

The wisdom shared was not intellectual but soulful. Each truth resonated deeply within, akin to notes on an ancient instrument awaiting discovery. These truths had long existed, buried beneath layers of experiences, perceptions, and conditioning. The universe had intricately intertwined them into my essence, awaiting the right moment and guidance for their emergence. As I listened, I recognized that these were not fresh insights but a long-forgotten reality—eternally present yet obscured—calling upon me to remember.

Embracing these revelations, I realized that they transcended mere theoretical concepts. They surpassed comprehension, reaching deep within my being and resonating with a truth that exceeded ordinary understanding. The mysteries of the universe, once veiled in uncertainty, revealed themselves vividly as I engaged with them fully. I understood that these truths had always existed, awaiting recognition, indicating that my journey was not about discovering new information but about remembering what I had already known. In the serene quietude of the jungle, next to the gently meandering river, I experienced peace in the realization of my unending connection to the Divine. The teachings revealed by Mother Ayahuasca align seamlessly with the ancient principles of the Vedic tradition, unveiling a profound truth: our essence is pure consciousness, within which the entire universe unfolds. Consciousness exists beyond the constraints of the material realm and manifests through two essential energies: Shiva and Shakti.

On the one hand, Shiva, regarded as the supreme cosmic force, embodies stillness and unchanging awareness. He is the eternal witness to all existence, observing without attachment and representing the peace that pervades the cosmos. On the other hand, Shakti embodies the Divine Feminine—the dynamic, creative energy that breathes life into the formless consciousness of Shiva. She represents the force that transforms the infinite into the tangible, infusing vibrancy into existence. Shakti propels all creation, manifesting movement and expression from Shiva's stillness. Together, they encompass the entirety of our being.

These two energies are not separate; they are inextricably linked, each one reliant on the other to complete the cosmic tapestry of life. The stillness of Shiva would be meaningless without Shakti's dynamism, just as Shakti's creativity necessitates the grounding of Shiva's awareness. Together, they illustrate the harmonious unity between the observer and the observed, the creator and the creation, the passive and the active. In this synergy, I realized that the universe is not fragmented but rather a cohesive expression of both stillness and movement.

Shiva is not an aloof deity but the pure, immutable core of awareness residing within us. He symbolizes profound stillness and eternal presence, an endless ocean of consciousness beneath the swirling currents of our thoughts and emotions. This awareness remains unaltered by the vicissitudes of life, akin to an infinite expanse that is consistently present, regardless of the surface storms.

When Mother Ayahuasca affirmed, "You are Shiva," it was neither an attempt to impose a title nor an identity upon me. Instead, it was an invitation to awaken to a deeper truth about my existence. It was a call to recognize the boundless essence within, transcending the limitations of the ego, desires that cloud perception, and fears that confine me. It served as a reminder that we are not defined by transient characteristics or experiences but by an unchanging consciousness that is perpetually present.

In a moment of such clarity, the false sense of isolation fades away. The perceived boundaries between ourselves and others, as well as between the self and the cosmos, dissolve. We no longer see ourselves as individuals opposing the world; instead, we become the silent observers of the unfolding narrative of life. The witness is not detached or passive; rather, it is fully engaged, perceiving with equanimity and free from judgment and attachment. Life's unfolding, with its triumphs and tribulations, is recognized as part of a larger stage to which we inherently belong.

To connect with the energy of Shiva means recognizing that we are not merely spectators of life; we are the very awareness through which existence is experienced. It signifies a state of profound peace and clarity, where the chaos of the mind ceases to dictate our perception of reality. In this state, we begin to align with the infinite presence that is our true nature, harmonizing with the universe—fully engaged yet unattached—and experiencing a deep sense of serenity.

For those who connect with the energy of Shakti, the experience is equally profound yet revealed through a dynamic lens. Shakti embodies the life force itself, the creative energy that breathes life into all existence. She is the divine spark coursing through our beings, enriching each moment with vitality and intent. This energy fuels our passions, drives our creativity, and urges us to nurture and transform our surroundings. It represents the creative pulse present in both the subtle details of daily life and the vast manifestations of the cosmos.

Shakti calls us to acknowledge the sanctity of all that exists. She encourages us to perceive the Divine within everything, viewing life as a sacred odyssey of transformation. Through Shakti, we grasp that every experience, every action, and every bond is a divine manifestation of the universe's boundless energy. There is no need to seek the Divine outside ourselves; it resides in every breath, thought, and movement. Life, with all its vibrancy and disorder, offers a gateway to connect with this sacred energy.

By embracing Shakti, we learn that the world is not a place to escape but a canvas for our souls unfolding. Every encounter, every act of creation, and each challenge we confront mirrors the divine energy in motion. We are called not to withdraw from existence but to engage fully, to create, heal, grow, and experience the depths of our essence. Shakti reveals that our life's purpose lies in actively participating in and celebrating the divine beauty surrounding us.

As we embody Shakti's energy, we realize that every action, no matter how trivial, presents an opportunity to articulate our divine essence. It is through Shakti that we uncover the interwoven nature of all things, understanding that we are not isolated from the world but are integral threads in the grand cosmic canvas. The flow of life reflects the Divine, and by opening ourselves to Shakti's energy, we discover that each moment invites us to live with heightened awareness, intention, and joy.

Living as Shiva entails cultivating a state of steadfast awareness—viewing the world through a lens of love and detachment. It signifies a sense of expansiveness and liberty, understanding that the fluctuations of life are simply waves in the immense sea of our existence. To be like Shiva is to remain anchored in unshakeable freedom, grounded in a tranquility that rises above the condition of duality.

On the other hand, embracing Shakti involves celebrating the creative force within us. It acknowledges our ability to enrich the world with beauty, healing, and transformation. Shakti fuels our ambitions and enables us to experience the depth of the universe entirely. In this mindset, every moment evolves into a sacred ceremony, and each interaction becomes a chance to manifest the Divine.

The journey with Mother Ayahuasca unveiled the profound truth that Shiva and Shakti are not ideals to achieve but essential states of awareness to rediscover. They are inherent facets of our being that, when recognized, seamlessly integrate into our lives. Shiva symbolizes deep, eternal calm—an awareness unaffected by the transient fluctuations of thought and emotion. It represents pure presence, the unyielding foundation of our existence that maintains equilibrium. Conversely, Shakti embodies the vibrant energy that flows through us, enlivening life with its creative and transformative essence. Together, Shiva and Shakti illustrate the entirety of our nature, demonstrating that we are both serenity and motion, quiet observers and active creators.

The deeper my journey with Ayahuasca unfolded, the clearer it became that this balance within us is not a goal to pursue but a realization to uncover. We are simultaneously Shiva and Shakti, the enduring awareness and dynamic energy intricately woven together. Grasping this truth is not merely an intellectual endeavor; it is an awakening to our inherent nature. As we align with both stillness and movement, we harmonize with the totality of existence, recognizing our integral role in the unfolding universe.

Such revelations transform our perspective on life. Rather than perceiving ourselves as isolated individuals navigating an indifferent universe, we come to recognize ourselves as expressions of divine consciousness. The same consciousness that permeates the cosmos also resides within us, allowing us to experience life in its myriad forms. We are no longer confined by the limitations of our ego or the illusion of separation that often colors our existence. Instead, we acknowledge our inseparability from the grand cosmic play.

By connecting to both Shiva and Shakti, we learn to coexist harmoniously with the forces shaping the universe. We no longer find ourselves ensnared in the duality of self and others; instead, we understand that our inner calm is intrinsically linked to the vibrant flow of existence. We are simultaneously observers and participants—those who experience and those who shape experience.

This comprehension alters our interaction with the world; where once we might have felt isolated or overwhelmed, we now cultivate a profound sense of unity and purpose.

The realization that we are not isolated entities but manifestations of divine consciousness reshapes our engagement with the world. Each moment becomes an opportunity to align with the broader flow of existence and to contribute to life's creation and transformation with grace and awareness. Acknowledging our divine nature empowers us to act with love, create with intention, and observe the world with profound insight. It is through recognizing Shiva and Shakti within us that we understand our true essence and the interconnection of all things.

Mother Ayahuasca's wisdom serves as an enlightening guide, demonstrating that the ultimate spiritual journey is one of integration. Genuine enlightenment arises from harmonizing Shiva and Shakti, permitting the stillness of Shiva to ground our actions and the vitality of Shakti to elevate our awareness. This divine equilibrium is not a distant aspiration but a lived reality—a way of being that honors both the silence and the melody of existence.

The wild splendor of the jungle reflected this harmony. The river, the trees, and the wildlife—all embody a shared awareness. The distinctions we perceive in the world are mere illusions. In reality, we are intricately linked, components of a grander unity. This insight carries a profound duty, as Don Howard articulated, "¡Para El Bien De Todos!"—for the welfare of all. Our awakening not only fosters individual growth but also nurtures the healing and elevation of every being. We are called to express our divine nature—to radiate love and light in a world that desperately seeks it.

Mother Ayahuasca has imparted the understanding that enlightenment is not a final destination but a continuous journey, an ever-deepening evolution. It is not a singular event but a persistent unfolding of our inner awareness, an ongoing expansion of understanding as we navigate life. Each moment invites us to deepen our connection to the Divine, revealing layers of sanctity woven into the fabric of reality. Enlightenment, as she teaches, embraces complete immersion in the present, engaging with the Divine play perpetually unfolding around and within us.

The path of enlightenment entails being present with all that surfaces—whether joy or sorrow, ease or challenge. It is a practice of living in continuous awareness, where every moment, regardless of its external manifestation, reflects the Divine. Every experience, from the ordinary to the extraordinary, holds the potential to awaken us further, deepening our understanding of interconnectivity. We begin to recognize that each moment is sacred, and each breath is a chance to return to the eternal now.

Embracing this perspective means accepting life as it unfolds without the urge to control or resist. It involves yielding to the universe's rhythm and recognizing that desires and fears are transient distractions, not the Ultimate Truth. Living in this awareness grants liberation, freeing us from the relentless pursuit of what lies ahead or the attachment to what we believe should be. It is about existing beyond the ego's constraints, firmly rooted in the present, where past regrets and future anxieties no longer dictate our reality.

This liberation emerges from within, not dictated by external situations. By embracing the wisdom of present-moment awareness, we discover that the eternal now is the sole reality, while everything else dissipates like smoke. In this understanding, we break free from the ego's constraints and the mind's distractions. We are allowed to embrace simplicity —to fully experience life as it unfolds and to connect with the Divine, both within us and in our surroundings, transcending the boundaries of time and space.

The Amazon, with its vast and untamed splendor, embraced me like a devoted guardian, offering a refuge that profoundly transformed me both physically and spiritually. The rich biodiversity revealed ancient knowledge, connecting me to the very spirit of the Earth. The truths to which I was granted access unearthed concealed dimensions of my being, allowing me to explore the intricacies of my life and the universe in ways I had previously deemed unattainable.

The jungle mirrored the divine consciousness I recognized in both Shiva and Shakti. The tranquility of Shiva lingered in the stillness between the rustling leaves and the flowing waters, harmonizing with the vibrant, creative force of Shakti that infused every living essence thriving in the jungle. This duality reflected my essence, and as I departed, I knew the jungle's energy would remain with me—ever-present and eternally vibrant.

Returning was not merely about re-entering the physical world; it represented a homecoming to my true self—to the inner space where I realized that all the answers I sought had always existed within me. The world would continue its course, and life would flow on, but I was irrevocably transformed. The jungle's wisdom, the sacred medicine, and the profound lessons taught by Mother Ayahuasca had opened my heart, awakened my spirit, and reaffirmed that everything I required was already within me.

Mother Ayahuasca's final message echoed deeply within me, urging me to embody unconditional love —not as a mere concept or belief but as a living, breathing truth. Her directive was unmistakable: to recognize the Divine in every being and to approach all life with compassion and empathy, regardless of the circumstances. Love transcends mere emotion; it is the energy that unites everything in existence, the highest truth that underpins all. It serves as the foundation of creation—the essence that weaves us together—because love is not a pursuit; it is a way of being.

The genuine work lies in how I choose to exist in the world, how I navigate life, how I relate to others, and how I nurture love within myself. It involves embracing the sacred in every act, in each word, and in every fleeting moment. To live as a testament to the Divine, demonstrating love through my very presence, is my sole purpose. This realization is about quietude, steadiness, and an open heart rather than seeking grandeur or acknowledgment.

Though the external world attempts to divert me in numerous ways, I know that, no matter where I roam, the love I have uncovered and now embody will serve as my guiding star. Mother Ayahuasca has imparted the knowledge of perceiving and embodying the Divine in all aspects of life. This marks my new way of existing: to be a vessel of love and to honor the sacred through my very being.

May you, beloved reader, carry this truth within your heart, embracing the profound understanding that you belong to something far greater than what appears around you. May you awaken to the divine spark dwelling within you and live in the radiance of love, compassion, and mindful awareness. Whether your journey leads you toward the serenity of Shiva or the dynamic energy of Shakti, understand that both express the same Eternal Truth. Each of us plays an essential role in this cosmic choreography—a dance that surpasses the confines of time, space, and form.

In the grand tapestry of existence, we are not separate, even though we may appear to be individual raindrops in an ocean. Our perceived separateness is ultimately an illusion, a veil created by the ego and the mind that obscures the profound unity of life. Beneath our surface lies the ocean of existence: limitless, eternal, and interconnected with everything. Each raindrop is integral to the whole, just as each of us is woven into the universe's fabric, coursing with the same divine energy.

While we navigate life as solitary beings, each with unique challenges, joys, and perspectives, the core of our being remains unified. We are all part of the same ocean, swaying in the same currents of existence. Our apparent separateness is merely an illusion, allowing us to explore life in its countless expressions. Beneath this façade, a deep, unbroken connection binds us. Each movement is guided by the same cosmic rhythm, whether we recognize it or not. We are dancers within the eternal performance, playing our roles in consciousness's grand play.

In this divine dance, there is no division; only Oneness exists. We are united by the same life energy, the same love, and the same eternal presence that flows through every living being, every star in the sky, and every breath we take. This is the Fundamental Truth. We are the ocean, we are the dance, we are love, and we are the infinite in which the flow of life unfolds. The illusion of separation is transient, but the Oneness that connects us remains eternal.

"¡Para El Bien De Todos!"

About the Author

The author is a research scientist, writer, and spiritual seeker who has spent much of his life exploring the crossroads of science, consciousness, and the mysteries of existence. He holds a PhD in Data Science, a Master's in Applied Physics, and a Bachelor's in Physics, and he has focused his academic work on understanding complex fields such as quantum computing and artificial intelligence, as well as their transformative applications in medical diagnostics. Despite these intellectual accomplishments, his quest for deeper meaning has remained at the core of his journey, driving him to seek answers to life's profound questions that extend beyond the confines of logic and reason.

After years of trying to understand the nature of reality and the purpose of existence, the author's path led him to the sacred teachings of Ayahuasca, a transformative medicine deeply revered by indigenous cultures in the Amazon. Through his experiences with Ayahuasca and his continued exploration of ancient spiritual traditions and modern physics, he has uncovered profound insights into the interconnectedness of all life and the play of divine consciousness. These experiences have begun to bridge the gaps between the mystical and the scientific, revealing a universal truth that binds all existence.

The inspiration to write *Mother Ayahuasca's Sacred Teachings: Unveiling Shiva: A Spiritual Quest Toward Enlightenment and Divine Oneness* arose from the transformative revelations that emerged during this journey. This book reflects the culmination of his spiritual odyssey, in which the lessons of Mother Ayahuasca unveiled not only the ancient wisdom of the Vedic traditions but also the profound interconnectedness of the universe, expressed through the divine energies of Shiva and Shakti. The book serves as both a memoir of his journey and a guide for those seeking spiritual awakening, self-realization, and an understanding of the deep truths that transcend our everyday experiences.

While the author shares his personal experiences, insights, and revelations, his intention is not to impose a belief system, religion, or worldview on anyone. Instead, he offers his journey as it unfolds —raw and unfiltered—hoping that others might find inspiration, understanding, or resonance in his encounters with the Divine. He honors all paths to truth, seeking only to contribute to the more extensive dialogue on self-discovery, spiritual growth, and the interconnectedness of all beings. Through this book, the author hopes to inspire others to embark on their journeys of exploration, healing, and spiritual awakening, realizing the limitless potential that resides within us all.

www.ingramcontent.com/pod-product-compliance
Lightning Source LLC
Chambersburg PA
CBHW050553170426
43201CB00011B/1685